Craiglist. org (also in $ post).
Rusrek. com
Bazar. club

yelp
Thumbtack
Handi.
TaScrabit

noyaball
зorelku
Xahghm

LinkedIn
ZipRecruiter

MW01290331

The Kazakh Dictionary

A Concise English-Kazakh Dictionary

By Alibek Berkumbaev

The Kazakh Dictionary

English-Kazakh Dictionary

English	Kazakh	Transliteration
A		
Aboard	Борт ішінде	Bort işinde
About	Туралы, жөнінде	Turalı, jöninde
Above	Жоғары	Joğarı
Accident	Апат	Apat
Account	Есеп, шот	Esep, şot
Across	Арқылы	Arqılı
Adapter	Адаптер, жалғастырғыш тетік	Adapter, jalğastırğış tetik
Address	Мекенжай	Mekenjay
Admit	Мойындау, кіру	Moyındau, kiru
Adult	Ересек	Eresek
Advice	Кеңес	Keñes
Afraid	Қорқу, қорыққан	Qorqu, qorıqqan
After	Кейін	Keyin
Age	Жас	Jas
Ago	Бұрын	Burın
Agree	Келісу	Kelisu
Ahead	Алға, ілгері	Alğa, ilgeri
Air	Ауа,әуе	Awa ,äwe
Air conditioning	Ауа салқындатқышы	Awa salqındatqışı
Airline	Әуе компаниясы	Äwe kompanïyası
Airplane	Ұшақ	Uşaq
Airport	Әуежай	Äwejay
Aisle	Дәліз, аралық, бөлік	Däliz , aralıq, bölik

1

English	Kazakh	Transliteration
A		
Alarm clock	Оятқыш	Oyatqış
Alcohol	Алкоголь, есірткіш	Alkogol', esirtkiş
All	Барлық	Barlıq
Allergy	Аллергия	Allergïya
Alone	Жалғыз	Jalğız
Already	Әлдеқашан	Äldeqaşan
Also	Сол сияқты	Sol sïyaqtı
Always	Әрдайым	Ärdayım
Ancient	Ежелгі	Ejelgi
And	Және	Jäne
Angry	Ызалы	Izalı
Animal	Жануар	Januar
Ankle	Тобық	Tobıq
Another	Басқа	Basqa
Answer	Жауап	Jauap
Antique	Антиктік, көне	Antïktik, köne
Apartment	Пәтер	Päter
Apple	Алма	Alma
Appointment	Кездесу, тағайындау	Kezdesu, tağayındau
Argue	Пікірталасу	Pikirtalasu
Arm	Алақан	Alaqan
Arrest	Тұтқындау	Tutqındau
Arrivals	Келуі	Kelui
Arrive	Келу	Kelu

English	Kazakh	Transliteration
A		
Art	Өнер	Öner
Artist	Әртіс	Ärtis
Ask (questinoning)	Сұрау	Surau
Ask (request)	Сауал	Sawal
Aspirin	Аспирин	Aspïrïn
At	Ішінде	Işinde
ATM	Банкомат	Bankomat
Awful	Қорқынышты	Qorqınıştı
B		
Baby	Бала	Bala
Babysitter	Бала күтуші	Bala kütuşi
Back (body)	Арқа	Arqa
Back (backward position)	Артында	Artında
Backpack	Иықкап, қолдорба	Ïïqqap, qoldorba
Bacon	Сүрсүбе	Sürsübe
Bad	Жаман	Jaman
Bag	Сөмке	Sömke
Baggage	Жүк	Jük
Baggage claim	Жүкті алу	Jükti alu
Bakery	Нан дүкені	Nan dükeni
Ball (sports)	Доп	Dop
Banana	Банан	Banan
Band (musician)	Топ (музыкалық)	Top (muzïkalıq)
Bandage	Орамал	Oramal

English	Kazakh	Transliteration
B		
Band-Aid	Жабысқақ пластырь	Jabısqaq plastır′
Bank	Банк	Bank
Bank account	Банк шоты	Bank şotı
Basket	Қоржын	Qorjın
Bath	Ванна	Vanna
Bathing suit	Шомылатын киім	Şomılatın kïim
Bathroom	Жуынатын бөлме	Juınatın bölme
Battery	Батарея	Batareya
Be	Болу	Bolu
Beach	Жағажай	Jağajay
Beautiful	Әдемі	Ädemi
Because	Өйткені	Öytkeni
Bed	Кереует	Kerewet
Bedroom	Ұйықтайтын бөлме	Uyıqtaytın bölme
Beef	Сиыр еті	Sïır eti
Beer	Сыра	Sıra
Before	Бұрын	Burın
Behind	Артында	Artında
Below	Астында, төменде	Astında, tömende
Beside	Қасында, жанында	Qasında, janında
Best	Өте жақсы	Öte jaqsı
Bet	Бәс салысу, бәстесу	Bäs salısu, bästesu
Between	Арасында	Arasında
Bicycle	Велосипед	Velosïped

English	Kazakh	Transliteration
B		
Big	Үлкен	Ülken
Bike	Велосипед	Velosïped
Bill (bill of sale)	Иелік қағаз	Ïelik qağaz
Bird	Құс	Qus
Birthday	Туған күн	Tuğan kün
Bite (dog bite)	Қабу	Qabu
Bitter	Ащы	Aşçı
Black	Қара	Qara
Blanket	Көрпе	Körpe
Blind	Соқыр	Soqır
Blood	Қан	Qan
Blue (dark blue)	Көк	Kök
Blue (light blue)	Ақшыл көк	Aqşıl kök
Board (climb aboard)	Бортқа міну	Bortqa minu
Boarding pass	Отырғызу талоны	Otırğızu talonı
Boat	Қайық	Qayıq
Body	Дене	Dene
Book	Кітап	Kitap
Bookshop	Кітап дүкені	Kitap dükeni
Boots (shoes)	Аяқ киімі	Ayaq kiïmi
Border	Пансионда тұрушы	Pansïonda turuşı
Bored	Сағынған, іші пысқан	Sağınğan, işi pısqan
Boring	Жалықтырғыш	Jalıqtırğış
Borrow	Қарызға алу	Qarızğa alu

English	Kazakh	Transliteration
B		
Both	Қос, екеуі де	Qos, ekewi de
Bottle	Бөтелке	Bötelke
Bottle opener (beer)	Бұранда	Buranda
Bottle opener (corkscrew)	Штопор	Ştopor
Bottom (butt)	Дүм, шүйде түбі	Düm, şüyde tübi
Bottom (on bottom)	Түбінде	Tübinde
Bowl	Ыдыс	Idıs
Box	Қорап	Qorap
Boy	Ұл	Ul
Boyfriend	Дос бала	Dos bala
Bra	Шам	Şam
Brave	Өжет	Öjet
Bread	Нан	Nan
Break	Бұзу	Buzu
Breakfast	Таңғы ас	Tañğı as
Breathe	Тыныс	Tınıs
Bribe	Қалыңдық	Qalıñdıq
Bridge	Көпір	Köpir
Bring	Алу	Alu
Broken (breaking)	Бұзылған, сынған (сыну)	Buzılğan, sınğan (sınu)
Brother	Дос	Dos
Brown	Қоңыр	Qoñır
Brush	Щётке	Şçyotke
Bucket	Шелек	Şelek

English	Kazakh	Transliteration
B		
Bug	Қате	Qate
Build	Құру	Quru
Builder	Құрылысшы	Qurılısşı
Building	Ғимарат	Ğïmarat
Burn	Жағу	Jağu
Bus	Автобус	Avtobus
Bus station	Автовокзал	Avtovokzal
Bus stop	Автобус аялдамасы	Avtobus ayaldaması
Business	Кәсіп	Käsip
Busy	Қол тимеу	Qol tïmew
But	Бірақ	Biraq
Butter	Май	May
Butterfly	Көбелек	Köbelek
Buy	Сатып алу	Satıp alu
C		
Cake (wedding cake)	Той торты	Toy tortı
Cake (birthday cake)	Туған күнге арналған торт	Tuğan künge arnalğan tort
Call	Шақыру	Şaqıru
Call (telephone call)	Телефон шалу	Telefon şalu
Camera	Камера	Kamera
Camp	Лагерь	Lager'
Campfire	Отын	Otın
Campsite	Жорық	Jorıq
Can (have the ability)	Қолдан келу, жасай алу	Qoldan kelu, jasay alu

English	Kazakh	Transliteration
C		
Can (allowed)	Мүмкін болу	Mümkin bolu
Can (aluminium can)	Қаңылтыр құты	Qañıltır qutı
Cancel	Болдырмау	Boldırmaw
Candle	Майшам	Mayşam
Candy	Кәмпит	Kämpït
Car	Автокөлік	Avtokölik
Cards (playing cards)	Ойын картасы	Oyın kartası
Care for	Бағу	Bağu
Carpenter	Ағаш шебері	Ağaş şeberi
Carriage	Тасымалдау	Tasımaldaw
Carrot	Сәбіз	Säbiz
Carry	Тасу	Tasu
Cash	Қолма-қол төлеу	Qolma-qol tölew
Cash (deposit a check)	Төлеу	Tölew
Cashier	Кассир	Kassir
Castle	Қорған	Qorğan
Cat	Мысық	Mısıq
Cathedral	Кафедралы собор	Kafedralı sobor
Celebration	Мерекелеу, тойлау	Merekelew, toylaw
Cell phone	Телефон	Telefon
Cemetery	Бейіт,зират	Beyit,zïrat
Cent	Цент	Cent
Centimeter	Сантиметр	Santïmetr
Center	Орталық	Ortalıq

English	Kazakh	Transliteration
C		
Cereal	Астық, ботқа	Astıq, botqa
Chair	Орындық	Orındıq
Chance	Мүмкіндік	Mümkindik
Change	Өзгеріс	Özgeris
Change (coinage)	Ұсақтау	Usaqtaw
Change (pocket change)	Алмастыру	Almastıru
Changin room	Киім ауыстыратын орын	Kïim awıstıratın orın
Chat up	Сөйлесу	Söylesu
Cheap	Арзан	Arzan
Cheat	Алдау	Aldaw
Cheese	Ірімшік	Irimşik
Chef	Басшы	Basşı
Cherry	Шие	Şïe
Chest (torso)	Кеуде, төс	Keude, tös
Chicken	Тауық еті	Tawıq eti
Child	Бала	Bala
Children	Балалар	Balalar
Chocolate	Шоколад	Şokolad
Choose	Таңдау	Tañdaw
Christmas	Рождество	Rojdestvo
Cider	Сидр	Sïdr
Cigar	Сигара	Sïgara
Cigarette	Шылым	Şılım
City	Қала	Qala

English	Kazakh	Transliteration
C		
City center	Қала орталығы	Qala ortalığı
Class (categorize)	Топ	Top
Clean	Таза	Taza
Cleaning	Тазалау	Tazalaw
Climb	Көтерілу	Köterilu
Clock	Сағат	Sağat
Close	Жабу	Jabu
Close (closer)	Жақын	Jaqın
Closed	Жабық	Jabıq
Clothing	Киіну	Kïinu
Clothing store	Киім дүкені	Kïim dükeni
Cloud	Бұлт	Bult
Cloudy	Бұлтты	Bulttı
Coast	Жаға, жағалау	Jağa, jağalaw
Coat	Пәлте	Pälte
Cockroach	Тарақан	Taraqan
Cocktail	Коктейль	Kokteyl'
Cocoa	Какао	Kakao
Coffee	Кофе	Kofe
Coins	Тиындар	Tïindar
Cold	Суық	Suıq
College	Колледж	Kolledj
Color	Түс	Tüs
Comb	Тарақ	Taraq

English	Kazakh	Transliteration
C		
Come	Келу	Kelu
Comfortable	Ыңғайлы	Iñğaylı
Compass	Компасс	Kompass
Complain	Арыз айту	Arız aytu
Complimentary (on the house)	Тегін	Tegin
Computer	Компьютер	Kompyuter
Concert	Концерт	Koncert
Conditioner (conditioning treatment)	Кондиционер (шашқа арналған)	Kondïcïoner (şaşqa arnalğan)
Contact lens solution	Жанаспалы линзалар ерітіндісі	Janaspalı lïnzalar eritindisi
Contact lenses	Жанаспалы линзалар	Janaspalı lïnzalar
Contract	Келісімшарт	Kelisimşart
Cook	Ас	As
Cookie	Печенье	Peçen'e
Cool (mild temperature)	Салқын	Salqın
Corn	Жүгері	Jügeri
Corner	Бұрыш	Burış
Cost	Баға	Bağa
Cotton	Мақта	Maqta
Cotton balls	Мақта дөңгелектері	Maqta döñgelekteri
Cough	Жөтел	Jötel
Count	Есептеу	Eseptew
Country	Ел	El

English	Kazakh	Transliteration
C		
Cow	Сиыр	Sïır
Crafts	Қолөнер	Qolöner
Crash	Апат	Apat
Crazy	Жынды	Jındı
Cream (creamy)	Крем	Krem
Cream (treatment)	Иісмай	Ïismay
Credit	Несие	Nesïe
Credit card	Несие картасы	Nesïe kartası
Cross (crucifix)	Керу	Keru
Crowded	Адамға лық толы	Adamǵa lıq tolı
Cruise	Круиз	Kruïz
Custom	Салт-дәстүр	Salt-dästür
Customs	Кеден	Keden
Cut	Қию	Qïyu
Cycle	Цикл	Cïkl
Cycling	Велосипед айдау	Velosïped aydaw
Cyclist	Велосипедші	Velosïpedşi
D		
Dad	Әке	Äke
Daily	Күнделікті	Kündelikti
Dance	Би	Bï
Dancing	Билеу	Bïlew
Dangerous	Қауіпті	Qauipti
Dark	Қараңғы	Qarańǵı

English	Kazakh	Transliteration
D		
Date (important notice)	Күн	Kün
Date (specific day)	Күн	Kün
Date (companion)	Кездесу	Kezdesu
Daughter	Қызы	Qızı
Dawn	Таң ату, басы	Tañ atu, bası
Day	Күн	Kün
Day after tomorrow	Арғы күн	Arğı kün
Day before yesterday	Алдыңғы күні	Aldıñğı küni
Dead	Өлген	Ölgen
Deaf	Керең, саңырау	Kereñ, sañıraw
Deal (card dealer)	Келісім	Kelisim
Decide	Шешу	Şeşu
Deep	Терең	Tereñ
Degrees (weather)	Градустар	Gradustar
Delay	Кідіріс, тұрып қалу	Kidiris, turıp qalu
Deliver	Жеткізу	Jetkizu
Dentist	Тіс дәрігері	Tis därigeri
Deodorant	Дезодарант	Dezodarant
Depart	Кету, артқа басу	Ketu, artqa basu
Department store	Әмбебап дүкені	Ämbebap dükeni
Departure	Ұшып кету	Uşıp ketu
Departure gate	Шығу қақпасы	Şığu qaqpası
Deposit	Депозит	Depozit
Desert	Десерт	Desert

English	Kazakh	Transliteration
D		
Dessert	Шөл	Şöl
Details	Бөлшектер	Bölşekter
Diaper	Жөргек	Jörgek
Diarrhea	Іш өту	Iş ötu
Diary	Күнделік	Kündelik
Die	Өлу, қайтып қалу	Ölu, qaytıp qalu
Diet	Диета	Dïeta
Different	Әртүрлі	Ärtürli
Difficult	Қиын	Qïın
Dinner	Түскі ас	Tüski as
Direct	Тура	Tura
Direction	Бағыт	Bağıt
Dirty	Лас	Las
Disaster	Апат	Apat
Disabled	Өшірілген, сөнген	Öşirilgen, söngen
Dish	Ыдыс	Idıs
Diving	Дайвинг	Dayvïng
Dizzy	Бас айналу	Bas aynalu
Do	Жасау	Jasaw
Doctor	Дәрігер	Däriger
Dog	Ит	Ït
Door	Есік	Esik
Double	Қос	Qos
Double bed	Қос кереует	Qos kerewet

English	Kazakh	Transliteration
D		
Double room	Қос бөлме	Qos bölme
Down	Төмен	Tömen
Downhill	Түсу, түсіру	Tüsu, tüsiru
Dream	Түс, арман	Tüs, arman
Dress	Көйлек	Köylek
Drink (cocktail)	Ішімдік	Işimdik
Drink (beverage)	Сусын	Susın
Drink	Ішу	Işu
Drive	Көлік жүргізу, айдау	Kölik jürgizu, aydaw
Drums	Дабыл, дағыра	Dabıl, dağıra
Drunk	Мас	Mas
Dry	Құрғақ	Qurğaq
Dry (warm up)	Кептіру	Keptiru
Duck	Үйрек	Üyrek
E		
Each	Әр	Är
Ear	Құлақ	Qulaq
Early	Ерте	Erte
Earn	Табыс табу	Tabıs tabu
East	Шығыс	Şığıs
Easy	Оңай, жеңіл	Oñay, jeñil
Eat	Жеу	Jew
Education	Білім, оқу	Bilim, oqu
Egg	Жұмыртқа	Jumırtqa

English	Kazakh	Transliteration
E		
Electricity	Электр желісі	Élektr jelisi
Elevator	Элеватор	Élevator
Embarrassed	Ұялған	Uyalğan
Emergency	Жедел	Jedel
Empty	Бос	Bos
End	Соңы	Soñı
English	Ағылшын	Ağılşın
Enjoy (enjoying)	Қызықтау	Qızıqtaw
Enough	Жеткілікті	Jetkilikti
Enter	Ену	Enu
Entry	Кіру	Kiru
Escalator	Эскалатор	Éskalator
Euro	Еуро	Euro
Evening	Кеш	Keş
Every	Әр	Är
Everyone	Әркім	Ärkim
Everything	Бәрі, барлығы	Bäri, barlığı
Exactly	Нақты	Naqtı
Exit	Шығу	Şığu
Expensive	Қымбат	Qımbat
Experience	Тәжірибе	Täjiribe
Eyes	Көздер	Közder
F		
Face	Бет, жүз	Bet, jüz

English	Kazakh	Transliteration
F		
Fall (autumnal)	Күз	Küz
Fall (falling)	Құлау	Qulaw
Family	Жанұя	Januya
Famous	Атақты	Ataqtı
Far	Алыс	Alıs
Fare	Қорқыныш	Qorqınış
Farm	Ферма	Ferma
Fast	Тез, жылдам	Tez, jıldam
Fat	Семіз	Semiz
Feel (touching)	Сезу	Sezu
Feelings	Сезімдер	Sezimder
Female	Әйел	Äyel
Fever	Қызу	Qızu
Few	Аз	Az
Fight	Төбелесу	Töbelesu
Fill	Толтыру	Toltıru
Fine	Тамаша	Tamaşa
Finger	Саусақ	Sausaq
Finish	Тоқтау	Toqtaw
Fire (heated)	От, алауошақ	Ot, alawoşaq
First	Бірінші	Birinşi
First-aid kit	Алғашқы көмек дәрі қорабы	Alğaşqı kömek däri qorabı
Fish	Балық	Balıq
Flat	Пәтер	Päter

English	Kazakh	Transliteration
F		
Floor (carpeting)	Еден	Eden
Floor (level)	Қатар	Qatar
Flour	Ұн	Un
Flower	Гүл	Gül
Fly	Ұшу	Uşu
Foggy	Тұман	Tuman
Follow	Артынан еру	Artınan eru
Food	Тамақ	Tamaq
Foot	Аяқ	Ayaq
Forest	Орман	Orman
Forever	Әрқашан	Ärqaşan
Forget	Ұмыту	Umıtu
Fork	Шанышқы	Şanışqı
Foul	Әділетсіз	Ädiletsiz
Fragile	Сынғыш	Sınğış
Free (at liberty)	Еркін	Erkin
Free (no cost)	Тегін	Tegin
Fresh	Балғын, жаңа	Balğın, jaña
Fridge	Тоңазытқыш	Toñazıtqış
Friend	Дос	Dos
From	-дан; -ден; -нан; -нен; -тан; -тен;	-dan; -den; -nan; -nen; -tan; -ten;
Frost	Аяз	Ayaz
Fruit	Жеміс	Jemis

18

English	Kazakh	Transliteration
F		
Fry	Қуыру	Quiru
Frying pan	Таба	Taba
Full	Толы	Tolı
Full-time	Толық қамтылу	Tolıq qamtılu
Fun	Қызық	Qızıq
Funny	Көңілді	Köñildi
Furniture	Жиһаз	Jïhaz
Future	Болашақ	Bolaşaq
G		
Game (match-up)	Жарыс	Jarıs
Game (event)	Ойын-сауық	Oyın-sawıq
Garbage	Қоқыс	Qoqıs
Garbage can	Қоқыс шелегі	Qoqıs şelegi
Garden	Бақша	Baqşa
Gas (gasoline)	Газ	Gaz
Gate (airport)	Қақпа	Qaqpa
Gauze	Дәке	Däke
Get	Алу	Alu
Get off (disembark)	Шығу, түсу	Şığu, tüsu
Gift	Сыйлық	Sıylıq
Girl	Қыз	Qız
Girlfriend	Дос қыз	Dos qız
Give	Беру	Beru
Glass	Стақан	Staqan

English	Kazakh	Transliteration
G		
Glasses (eyeglasses)	Көзілдірік	Közildirik
Gloves	Қолғап	Qolğap
Glue	Желім	Jelim
Go (walk)	Серуендеу	Seruendew
Go (drive)	Айдау	Aydaw
Go out	Үйден шығу	Üyden şiğu
God (deity)	Құдай	Quday
Gold	Алтын	Altın
Good	Жақсы	Jaqsı
Government	Мемлекет	Memleket
Gram	Грамм	Gramm
Granddaughter	Немере қыз	Nemere qız
Grandfather	Ата	Ata
Grandmother	Әже	Äje
Grandson	Немере ұл	Nemere ul
Grass	Шөп	Şöp
Grateful	Игілікті	Ïgilikti
Grave	Зират	Zïrat
Great (wonderful)	Ұлы	Ulı
Green	Жасыл	Jasıl
Grey	Сұры	Surı
Grocery	Азық-түлік	Azıq-tülik
Grow	Өсу	Ösu
Guaranteed	Кепілді	Kepildi

English	Kazakh	Transliteration
G		
Guess	Жобалау, ойлау	Jobalaw, oylaw
Guilty	Кінәлі	Kinäli
Guitar	Гитара	Gïtara
Gun	Қару, мылтық	Qaru, mıltıq
Gym	Спорт залы	Sport zalı
H		
Hair	Шаш	Şaş
Hairbrush	Тарақ	Taraq
Haircut	Шаш алдыру	Şaş aldıru
Half	Жарты	Jartı
Hand	Қол	Qol
Handbag	Қолдорба	Qoldorba
Handkerchief	Қол орамал	Qol oramal
Handmade	Қолдан жасалған	Qoldan jasalğan
Handsome	Әдемі	Ädemi
Happy	Бақытты	Baqıttı
Hard (firm)	Қатты	Qattı
Hard-boiled	Қатты қайнатылған, пісірілген	Qattı qaynatılğan, pisirilgen
Hat	Қалпақ	Qalpaq
Have	Бар	Bar
Have a cold	Суық тию	Suıq tïyu
Have fun	Көңіл көтеру	Köñil köteru
He	Ол	Ol
Head	Бас	Bas

English	Kazakh	Transliteration
H		
Headache	Бас ауыру	Bas auıru
Headlights	Шамдар	Şamdar
Health	Денсаулық	Densawlıq
Hear	Есту	Estu
Heart	Жүрек	Jürek
Heat	Жоғары температура	Joğarı temperatura
Heated	Жылыту	Jılıtu
Heater	Жылытқыш	Jılıtqış
Heavy	Ауыр	Auır
Helmet	Дулыға	Dulığa
Help	Көмек	Kömek
Her (hers)	Оның, онікі	Onıñ, oniki
Herb	Шөп	Şöp
Herbal	Шөпті	Şöpti
Here	Мұнда	Munda
High (steep)	Жоғары	Joğarı
High school	Орта мектеп	Orta mektep
Highway	Тас жол	Tas jol
Hike	Саяхат	Sayaxat
Hiking	Жаяу саяхат	Jayaw sayaxat
Hill	Төбе	Töbe
Hire	Жұмысқа алу	Jumısqa alu
His	Оның	Onıñ
History	Тарих	Tarïx

English	Kazakh	Transliteration
H		
Holiday	Мереке	Mereke
Holidays	Демалыс күндері	Demalıs künderi
Home	Үй	Üy
Honey	Бал	Bal
Horse	Жылқы	Jılqı
Hospital	Аурухана	Auruxana
Hot	Ыстық	Istıq
Hot water	Ыстық су	Istıq su
Hotel	Қонақ үй	Qonaq üy
Hour	Бір сағат	Bir sağat
House	Үй	Üy
How	Қалай	Qalay
How much	Қанша	Qanşa
Hug	Құшақ	Quşaq
Humid	Ылғал	Ilğal
Hungry (famished)	Аш	Aş
Hurt	Ауырту	Auırtu
Husband	Күйеу	Küyew
I		
Ice	Мұз	Muz
Ice cream	Балмұздақ	Balmuzdaq
Identification	Куәлік	Kuälik
ID card	Куәландыру картасы	Kuälandıru kartası
Idiot	Есуас	Esuas

English	Kazakh	Transliteration
I		
If	Егер	Eger
Ill	Ауыру, науқас болу	Auıru, nauqas bolu
Important	Маңызды	Mañızdı
Impossible	Мүмкін емес	Mümkin emes
In	Ішінде	Işinde
(be) in a hurry	Асығу	Asığu
In front of	Алдында	Aldında
Included	Енгізілген	Engizilgen
Indoor	Ғимарат ішінде	Ğimarat işinde
Information	Ақпарат	Aqparat
Ingredient	Ингредиент	Ïngredïent
Injury	Жарақат	Jaraqat
Innocent	Жазықсыз, пәк	Jazıqsız, päk
Inside	Ішінде	Işinde
Interesting	Қызықты	Qızıqtı
Invite	Шақыру	Şaqıru
Island	Арал	Aral
It	Бұл	Bul
Itch	Қышу	Qışu
J		
Jacket	Күрте	Kürte
Jail	Түрме	Türme
Jar	Ыдыс	Idıs
Jaw	Жақ	Jaq

English	Kazakh	Transliteration
J		
Jeep	Джип	Jïp
Jewelry	Зергерлік бұйымдар	Zergerlik buyımdar
Job	Жұмыс	Jumıs
Jogging	Жүгіру	Jügiru
Joke	Қалжың, әзіл	Qaljıñ, äzil
Juice	Шырын	Şırın
Jumper (cardigan)	Жемпір, тоқыма киім	Jempir, toqıma kïim
K		
Key	Кілт	Kilt
Keyboard	Пернетақта	Pernetaqta
Kilogram	Килограмм	Kïlogramm
Kilometer	Шақырым	Şaqırım
Kind (sweet)	Мырза	Mırza
Kindergarten	Бала бақша	Bala baqşa
King	Патша	Patşa
Kiss	Сүю	Süyu
Kiss	Безе	Beze
Kitchen	Ас бөлмесі	As bölmesi
Knee	Тізе	Tize
Knife	Пышақ	Pışaq
Know	Білім	Bilim
L		
Lace	Шілтер	Şilter
Lake	Өзен	Özen

English	Kazakh	Transliteration
L		
Land	Жер	Jer
Language	Тіл	Til
Laptop	Ноутбук	Noutbuk
Large	Үлкен	Ülken
Last (finale)	Соңғы	Soñğı
Last (previously)	Әуелгі	Äwelgi
Law (edict)	Заң, құқық	Zañ, quqıq
Lawyer	Заңгер	Zañger
Lazy	Еріншек	Erinşek
Leader	Қолбасшы	Qolbasşı
Learn	Үйрену	Üyrenu
Leather	Тері	Teri
Left (leftward)	Сол, сол жақ	Sol, sol jaq
Leg	Аяқ	Ayaq
Legal	Заңды	Zañdı
Lemon	Лимон	Limon
Lemonade	Лимонад	Limonad
Lens	Обьектив	Ob'ektïv
Lesbian	Лесбияндық	Lesbïyandıq
Less	Аз	Az
Letter (envelope)	Хат	Xat
Lettuce	Салат	Salat
Liar	Өтірікші	Ötirikşi
Library	Кітапхана	Kitapxana

English	Kazakh	Transliteration
L		
Lie (lying)	Жату	Jatu
Lie (falsehood)	Өтірік айту	Ötirik aytu
Life	Өмір	Ömir
Light	Жарық	Jarıq
Light (pale)	Жарық (бозғылт)	Jarıq (bozğılt)
Light (weightless)	Жеңіл (салмақсыз)	Jeñil (salmaqsız)
Light bulb	Кішкентай шам	Kişkentay şam
Lighter (ignited)	Оттық, шақпақ	Ottıq, şaqpaq
Like	Секілді, ұқсас	Sekildi, uqsas
Lime	Лайм	Laym
Lips	Ерін	Erin
Lipstick	Ерін далабы	Erin dalabı
Liquor store	Ликёрлі-арақ зауыты	Lïkyorli-araq zauıtı
Listen	Тыңдау	Tıñdaw
Little (few)	Бірнеше	Birneşe
Little (tiny)	Кіп-кішкентай	Kip-kişkentay
Live (occupy)	Өмір сүру	Ömir süru
Local	Жергілікті	Jergilikti
Lock	Құлып	Qulıp
Locked	Бекітулі	Bekituli
Long	Ұзын	Uzın
Look	Қарау	Qaraw
Look for	Іздеу	Izdew
Lose	Жоғалту	Joğaltu

English	Kazakh	Transliteration
L		
Lost	Жоғалған	Joğalğan
Lot	Көп	Köp
Loud	Күшті, қатты	Küşti, qattı
Love	Махаббат	Maxabbat
Low	Төмен	Tömen
Luck	Сәттілік	Sättilik
Lucky	Сәтті	Sätti
Luggage	Жүк	Jük
Lump	Сең, үйінді	Señ, üyindi
Lunch	Түскі ас	Tüski as
Luxury	Молшылық, байлық	Molşılıq, baylıq
M		
Machine	Машина	Maşïna
Magazine	Журнал	Jurnal
Mail (mailing)	Пошта (пошталық)	Poşta (poştalıq)
Mailbox	Пошта жәшігі	Poşta jäşigi
Main	Негізгі	Negizgi
Mainroad	Негізгі жол	Negizgi jol
Make	Жасау	Jasaw
Make-up	Біріктіру	Biriktiru
Man	Ер адам	Er adam
Many	Көп,көптеген	Köp,köptegen
Map	Карта	Karta
Market	Базар, нарық	Bazar, narıq

English	Kazakh	Transliteration
M		
Marriage	Тұрмыс құру	Turmıs quru
Marry	Үйлену	Üylenu
Matches (matchbox)	Сіріңке	Siriñke
Mattress	Матрас	Matras
Maybe	Мүмкін болу	Mümkin bolu
Me	Мен	Men
Meal	Ас	As
Meat	Ет	Et
Medicine (medicinals)	Медицина	Medïcïna
Meet	Кездесу	Kezdesu
Meeting	Кездесу	Kezdesu
Member	Мүше	Müşe
Message	Хабар, хат	Xabar, xat
Metal	Металл	Metall
Meter	Метр	Metr
Microwave	Қысқа толқынды пеш	Qısqa tolqındı peş
Midday	Түс кезі	Tüs kezi
Midnight	Түн ортасы	Tün ortası
Military	Әскери	Äskerï
Milk	Сүт	Süt
Millimeter	Миллиметр	Mïllïmetr
Minute (moment)	Минут	Mïnut
Mirror	Айна	Ayna
Miss (lady)	Ханым	Xanım

English	Kazakh	Transliteration
M		
Miss (mishap)	Сәтсіздік	Sätsizdik
Mistake	Қателік	Qatelik
Mobile phone	Ұялы телефон	Uyalı telefon
Modern	Заманауи	Zamanauï
Money	Ақша	Aqşa
Month	Ай	Ay
More	Көбірек	Köbirek
Morning	Таң	Tañ
Mosquito	Маса	Masa
Motel	Қонақ үй	Qonaq üy
Mother	Ана	Ana
Mother-in-law	Ене	Ene
Motorbike	Мотоцикл	Motocïkl
Motorboat	Моторлы қайық	Motorlı qayıq
Mountain	Тау	Taw
Mountain range	Тау жотасы	Taw jotası
Mouse	Тышқан	Tışqan
Mouth	Ауыз	Awız
Movie	Кино	Kïno
Mr.	Мырза	Mırza
Mrs./Ms	Ханым	Xanım
Mud	Балшық	Balşıq
Murder	Өлтіру	Öltiru
Muscle	Бұлшықет	Bulşıqet

English	Kazakh	Transliteration
M		
Museum	Мұражай	Murajay
Music	Музыка	Muzıka
Mustard	Қыша	Qışa
Mute	Мылқау	Mılqaw
My	Менің	Meniñ
N		
Nail clippers	Тырнақ тістеуігі	Tırnaq tistewigi
Name (moniker)	Лақап ат	Laqap at
Name (term)	Аты	Atı
Name (surname)	Аты-жөні	Atı-jöni
Napkin	Майлық	Maylıq
Nature	Табиғат	Tabiğat
Nausea	Жүрек айну	Jürek aynu
Near (close)	Жақын	Jaqın
Nearest	Ең жақын	Eñ jaqın
Necessity	Қажеттілік	Qajettilik
Neck	Мойын	Moyın
Necklace	Алқа	Alqa
Need	Қажеттілік	Qajettilik
Needle (stitch)	Ине	Ïne
Negative	Теріс, жағымғыз	Teris, jağımğız
Neither...nor...	Да; де	Da; de
Net	Тор, желі	Tor, jeli
Never	Ешқашан	Eşqaşan

31

English	Kazakh	Transliteration
N		
New	Жаңа	Jaña
News	Жаңалықтар	Jañalıqtar
Newspaper	Газет	Gazet
Next (ensuing)	Келесі	Kelesi
Next to	Қасында, жақын	Qasında, jaqın
Nice	Жақсы, сүйкімді	Jaqsı, süykimdi
Nickname	Жалған ат	Jalğan at
Night	Түн	Tün
Nightclub	Түнгі клуб	Tüngi klub
No	Жоқ	Joq
Noisy	Шулы	Şulı
None	Ешбір	Eşbir
Nonsmoking	Шылым шегуге болмайды	Şılım şeguge bolmaydı
Noon	Түс кезі	Tüs kezi
North	Солтүстік	Soltüstik
Nose	Мұрын	Murın
Not	Емес; -ба; -бе; -ма; -ме; -па; -пе;	Emes; -ba; -be; -ma; -me; -pa; -pe;
Notebook	Дәптерше	Däpterşe
Nothing	Ештеңе	Eşteñe
Now	Қазір	Qazir
Number	Нөмір	Nömir
Nurse	Мейірбике	Meyirbïke
Nut	Жаңғақ	Jañğaq

English	Kazakh	Transliteration
O		
Ocean	Мұхит	Muxït
Off (strange)	Біртүрлі	Birtürli
Office	Кеңсе	Keñse
Often	Жиі	Jïi
Oil (oily)	Май (майлы)	May (maylı)
Old	Ескі	Eski
On	Үстінде	Üstinde
On time	Уақытында	Waqıtında
Once	Бір рет	Bir ret
One	Бір	Bir
One-way	Бір бағытта	Bir bağıtta
Only	Тек қана	Tek qana
Open	Ашық	Aşıq
Operation (process)	Операция	Operacïya
Operator	Оператор	Operator
Opinion	Пікір	Pikir
Opposite	Қарсы	Qarsı
Or	Немесе	Nemese
Orange (citrus)	Апельсин	Apel'sïn
Orange (color)	Қызғылт сары	Qızğılt sarı
Orchestra	Оркестр	Orkestr
Order	Тапсырыс	Tapsırıs
Order	Бұйрық	Buyrıq
Ordinary	Әдеттегідей	Ädettegidey
Original	Түпкі	Tüpki
Other	Басқа	Basqa

English	Kazakh	Transliteration
O		
Our	Біздің	Bizdiñ
Outside	Сыртқа	Sırtqa
Oven	Пеш	Peş
Overnight	Түні бойы	Tüni boyı
Overseas	Шетел	Şetel
Owner	Иегер	Ïeger
Oxygen	Оттегі	Ottegi
P		
Package	Қаптама	Qaptama
Packet	Бума, пакет	Buma, paket
Padlock	Құлып	Qulıp
Page	Бет	Bet
Pain	Ауыру	Auıru
Painful	Аурушаң, ауыратын	Auruşañ, auıratın
Painkiller	Ауырғанды басатын	Auırğandı basatın
Painter	Суретші	Suretşi
Painting (canvas)	Сурет	Suret
Painting (the art)	Сурет өнері	Suret öneri
Pair	Қос, жұп	Qos, jup
Pan	Кәстрөл	Käströl
Pants (slacks)	Шалбар	Şalbar
Paper	Қағаз	Qağaz
Paperwork	Жазба жұмысы	Jazba jumısı
Parents	Ата-ана	Ata-ana

English	Kazakh	Transliteration
P		
Park	Саябақ	Sayabaq
Park (parking)	Паркинг	Parking
Part (piece)	Бөлік, тілім	Bölik, tilim
Part-time	Ішінара	Işinara
Party (celebration)	Той	Toy
Party (political)	Партия	Partïya
Pass	Тапсыру	Tapsıru
Passenger	Жолаушы	Jolawşı
Passport	Паспорт	Pasport
Past (ago)	Өткен	Ötken
Path	Жол	Jol
Pay	ойнау	oynaw
Payment	Төлем	Tölem
Peace	Бейбітшілік	Beybitşilik
Peach	Шабдалы	Şabdalı
Peanut	Жержаңғақ	Jerjañğaq
Pear	Алмұрт	Almurt
Pedal	Педаль	Pedal'
Pedestrian	Жаяу жүруші	Jayaw jüruşi
Pen	Қалам	Qalam
Pencil	Қаламсап	Qalamsap
People	Адамдар	Adamdar
Pepper (peppery)	Ащы бұрыш	Aşçı burış
Per	-да; -де; -та; -те	-da; -de; -ta; -te

English	Kazakh	Transliteration
P		
Per cent	Пайыз	Payız
Perfect	Мінсіз	Minsiz
Performance	Көрініс	Körinis
Perfume	Иіссу	Ïissu
Permission (permit)	Рұқсат	Ruqsat
Person	Адам	Adam
Petrol	Бензин	Benzïn
Petrol station	Жанармай құю станциясы	Janarmay quyu stancïyası
Pharmacy	Дәріхана	Därixana
Phone book	Телефон кітапшасы	Telefon kitapşası
Photo	Фотосурет	Fotosuret
Photographer	Фотограф	Fotograf
Pigeon	Көгершін	Kögerşin
Pie	Бәліш	Bäliş
Piece	Тілім, бөлік	Tilim, bölik
Pig	Шошқа	Şoşqa
Pill	Таблетка	Tabletka
Pillow	Жастық	Jastıq
Pillowcase	Жастық тысы	Jastıq tısı
Pink	Қызғылт	Qızğılt
Place	Орын	Orın
Plane	Ұшқыш	Uşqış
Planet	Ғаламшар	Ğalamşar
Plant	Өсімдік	Ösimdik

English	Kazakh	Transliteration
P		
Plastic	Пластик	Plastïk
Plate	Тәрелке	Tärelke
Play (strum)	Ойнау, тарту	Oynaw, tartu
Play (theatrical)	Пьеса	P'esa
Plug (stopper)	Тығын	Tığın
Plug (socket)	Штепсель	Ştepsel'
Plum	Өрік	Örik
Pocket	Қалта	Qalta
Point	Нүкте	Nükte
Poisonous	Улы	Ulı
Police	Полицей	Polïcey
Police officer	Полиция офицері	Polïcïya ofïceri
Police station	Полиция бөлімі	Polïcïya bölimi
Politics	Саясат	Sayasat
Pollution	Ластану	Lastanu
Pool (basin)	Хауыз	Xawız
Poor	Кедей	Kedey
Popular	Атақты	Ataqtı
Pork	Шошқа еті	Şoşqa eti
Port (dock)	Кемежай	Kemejay
Positive	Жақсы, оң	Jaqsı, oñ
Possible	Мүмкін болу	Mümkin bolu
Postcard	Ашық хат	Aşıq xat
Post office	Пошта бөлімі	Poşta bölimi

English	Kazakh	Transliteration
P		
Pot (kettle)	Шәйнек	Şäynek
Potato	Картоп	Kartop
Pottery	Күйіктас	Küyiktas
Pound (ounces)	Қадақ	Qadaq
Poverty	Кедейлік	Kedeylik
Powder	Ұнтақ	Untaq
Power	Қуаттылық, күш	Quattılıq, küş
Prayer	Дұға оқу	Duğa oqu
Prefer	Қалау	Qalaw
Pregnant	Жүкті болу	Jükti bolu
Prepare	Дайындау	Dayındaw
Prescription	Рецепт	Recept
Present (treat)	Сыйлық	Sıylıq
Present (now)	Осы шақ	Osı şaq
President	Президент, елбасы	Prezïdent, elbası
Pressure	Қысым	Qısım
Pretty	Сүйкімді	Süykimdi
Price	Баға	Bağa
Priest	Молда	Molda
Printer (printing)	Принтер	Prïnter
Prison	Түрме	Türme
Private	Жеке	Jeke
Produce	Өндіру	Öndiru
Profit	Кіріс, пайда	Kiris, payda

English	Kazakh	Transliteration
P		
Program	Бағдарлама	Bağdarlama
Promise	Сөз беру	Söz beru
Protect	Қорғау	Qorğaw
Pub	Паб	Pab
Public toilet	Қоғамдық дәретхана	Qoğamdıq däretxana
Pull	Тарту	Tartu
Pump	Сорғыш	Sorğış
Pumpkin	Асқабақ	Asqabaq
Pure	Таза, қоспасыз	Taza, qospasız
Purple	Қызылкүрең	Qızılküreñ
Purse	Әмиян	Ämïyan
Push	Басу, итеру	Basu, ïteru
Put	Салу, қою	Salu, qoyu
Q		
Quality	Сапа	Sapa
Quarter	Ширек	Şïrek
Queen	Патшайым	Patşayım
Question	Сұрақ	Suraq
Queue	Кезек	Kezek
Quick	Тез, лезде	Tez, lezde
Quiet	Тыныш	Tınış
Quit	Босатылу	Bosatılu
R		
Rabbit	Қоян	Qoyan

English	Kazakh	Transliteration
R		
Race (running)	Жарыс	Jarıs
Radiator	Радиатор	Radïator
Radio	Радио	Radïo
Rain	Жаңбыр	Jañbır
Raincoat	Плащ	Plaşç
Rare (exotic)	Сирек кездесетін	Sïrek kezdesetin
Rare (unique)	Ерекше, өзгеше	Erekşe, özgeşe
Rash	Бөртпе	Börtpe
Raspberry	Таңқурай	Tañquray
Rat	Егеуқұйрық	Egeuquyrıq
Raw	Шикізат	Şïkizat
Razor	Ұстара	Ustara
Read	Оқу	Oqu
Reading	Оқу	Oqu
Ready	Дайын болу	Dayın bolu
Rear (behind)	Артқы	Artqı
Reason	Себеп	Sebep
Receipt	Түбіртек	Tübirtek
Recently	Соңғы уақытта	Soñğı waqıtta
Recomment	Ұсыну	Usınu
Record (music)	Музыка жазу	Muzıka jazu
Recycle	Қайта өңдеу	Qayta öñdew
Red	Қызыл	Qızıl
Refrigerator	Тоңазытқыш	Toñazıtqış

English	Kazakh	Transliteration
R		
Refund	Қайтару	Qaytaru
Refuse	Бас тарту	Bas tartu
Regret	Өкіну	Ökinu
Relationship	Қарым-қатынас	Qarım-qatınas
Relax	Босаңсу	Bosañsu
Relic	Атамұра	Atamura
Religion	Дін	Din
Religious	Діни	Dinï
Remote	Дистанциялық пульт	Dïstancïyalıq pul't
Rent	Жалдау	Jaldaw
Repair	Жөндеу	Jöndew
Reservation (reserving)	Брондау	Brondaw
Rest	Демалыс	Demalıs
Restaurant	Мейрамхана	Meyramxana
Return (homecoming)	Елге оралу	Elge oralu
Return (returning)	Қайта оралу	Qayta oralu
Review	Шолу	Şolu
Rhythm	Ырғақ	Irğaq
Rib	Қабырға	Qabırğa
Rice	Күріш	Küriş
Rich (prosperous)	Бай	Bay
Ride	Сапар	Sapar
Ride (riding)	Ат мініп жүру	At minip jüru
Right (appropriate)	Құқық	Quqıq

English	Kazakh	Transliteration
R		
Right (rightward)	Оңға	Oñğa
Ring (bauble)	Сақина	Saqïna
Ring (ringing)	Қоңырау	Qoñıraw
Rip-off	Тонау, алаяқтық	Tonaw, alayaqtıq
River	Өзен	Özen
Road	Жол	Jol
Rob	Тонау	Tonaw
Robbery	Тонаушылық	Tonawşılıq
Rock	Рок, жазмыш	Rok, jazmış
Romantic	Романтикалық	Romantïkalıq
Room (accommodation)	Қонақүй нөмірі	Qonaqüy nömiri
Room (chamber)	Аурухана бөлмесі	Awruxana bölmesi
Room number	Нөмір саны	Nömir sanı
Rope	Жіп	Jip
Round	Дөңгелек	Döñgelek
Route	Бағдар	Bağdar
Rug	Кілем	Kilem
Ruins	Қираған үйінді	Qïrağan üyindi
Rule	Ереже	Ereje
Rum	Ром	Rom
Run	Жүгіру	Jügiru
Running	Жүгіріс	Jügiris
Sad	Көңілсіз	Köñilsiz
Safe	Қауіпсіз	Qawipsiz

English	Kazakh	Transliteration
S		
Salad	Салат	Salat
Sale (special)	Жаппай сатылым	Jappay satılım
Sales tax	Сатылым салығы	Satılım salığı
Salmon	Албырт	Albırt
Salt	Тұз	Tuz
Same	Бірдей	Birdey
Sand	Құм	Qum
Sandal	Сандал	Sandal
Sauce	Тұздық	Tuzdıq
Saucepan	Кәстрөл	Käströl
Sauna	Монша	Monşa
Say	Айту	Aytu
Scarf	Мойынорағыш	Moyınorağış
School	Мектеп	Mektep
Science	Ғылым	Ğılım
Scientist	Ғалым	Ğalım
Scissors	Қайшы	Qayşı
Sea	Теңіз	Teñiz
Seasickness	Теңіз ауруы	Teñiz awruı
Season	Жыл мезгілі	Jıl mezgili
Seat	Орындық	Orındıq
Seatbelt	Қауіпсіздік белдемшесі	Qawipsizdik beldemşesi
Second (moment)	Екіншіден	Ekinşiden
Second	Екінші	Ekinşi

English	Kazakh	Transliteration
S		
See	Көру	Köru
Selfish	Өзімшіл	Özimşil
Sell	Сату	Satu
Send	Жіберу	Jiberu
Sensible	Парасатты, ақылды	Parasattı, aqıldı
Sensual	Сезімтал	Sezimtal
Seperate	Бөлек	Bölek
Serious	Салмақты	Salmaqtı
Service	Қызмет көрсету	Qızmet körsetu
Several	Бірнеше	Birneşe
Sew	Тігу	Tigu
Sex	Секс	Seks
Sexism	Сексизм	Seksїzm
Sexy	Сексуалды	Seksualdı
Shade (shady)	Көлеңке	Köleñke
Shampoo	Сусабын	Susabın
Shape	Жағдай	Jağday
Share (sharing)	Үлес	Üles
Share (allotment)	Бөлік	Bölik
Shave	Қыру, қырыну	Qıru, qırınu
Shaving cream	Қырынуға арналған иісмай	Qırınuğa arnalğan iismay
She	Ол	Ol
Sheet (linens)	Төсек жайма	Tösek jayma
Ship	Кеме	Keme

English	Kazakh	Transliteration
S		
Shirt	Жейде, көйлек	Jeyde, köylek
Shoes	Аяқ киім	Ayaq kiim
Shoot	Ату	Atu
Shop	Дүкен	Düken
Shop	Кәсіпорын	Käsiporın
Shopping center	Сауда орталығы	Sawda ortalığı
Short (low)	Қысқа	Qısqa
Shortage	Тапшылық	Tapşılıq
Shorts	Шолақ шалбар	Şolaq şalbar
Shoulder	Иық	Ïıq
Shout	Айқай	Ayqay
Show	Көрсету	Körsetu
Show	Көрме	Körme
Shower	Душ, жауын	Duş, jawın
Shut	Жабу	Jabu
Shy	Ұялшақ	Uyalşaq
Sick	Науқас	Nawqas
Side	Жаны, жағы	Janı, jağı
Sign	Белгі	Belgi
Sign (signature)	Қол қою	Qol qoyu
Signature	Қол қойылу	Qol qoyılu
Silk	Жібек	Jibek
Silver	Күміс	Kümis
Similar	Бірдей	Birdey

English	Kazakh	Transliteration
S		
Simple	Жай, қарапайым	Jay, qarapayım
Since	Бері	Beri
Sing	Ән айту	Än aytu
Singer	Әнші	Änşi
Single (individual)	Жалғыз	Jalğız
Sister	Апа	Apa
Sit	Отыру	Otıru
Size (extent)	Өлшем	Ölşem
Skin	Тері	Teri
Skirt	Белдемше, юбка	Beldemşe, yubka
Sky	Аспан	Aspan
Sleep	Ұйықтау	Uyıqtaw
Sleepy	Ұйқылы	Uyqılı
Slice	Тілім, үзім	Tilim, üzim
Slow	Бәсең	Bäseñ
Slowly	Асықпай	Asıqpay
Small	Кішкентай	Kişkentay
Smell	Иіс	Ïis
Smile	Күлімсіреу	Külimsirew
Smoke	Түтін	Tütin
Snack	Дәмтатым	Dämtatım
Snake	Жылан	Jılan
Snow	Қар	Qar
Soap	Сабын	Sabın

English	Kazakh	Transliteration
S		
Socks	Шұлықтар	Şulıqtar
Soda	Содалы су	Sodalı su
Soft-drink	Алкогольсіз сусын	Alkogol'siz susın
Some	Біршама	Birşama
Someone	Әлдебіреу	Äldebirew
Something	Бір нәрсе	Bir närse
Son	Ұл	Ul
Song	Ән	Än
Soon	Жақын арада	Jaqın arada
Sore	Жарақат	Jaraqat
Soup	Сорпа, көже	Sorpa, köje
South	Оңтүстік	Oñtüstik
Specialist	Маман	Maman
Speed (rate)	Жылдамдық	Jıldamdıq
Spinach	Саумалдық	Sawmaldıq
Spoiled (rotten)	Бұзылған	Buzılğan
Spoke	Айтылған	Aytılğan
Spoon	Қасық	Qasıq
Sprain	Сіңір созылуы	Siñir sozıluı
Spring (prime)	Көктем	Köktem
Square (town center)	Алаң	Alañ
Stadium	Стадион	Stadion
Stamp	Марка	Marka
Star	Жұлдыз	Juldız

English	Kazakh	Transliteration
S		
Star sign	Жұлдыз белгісі	Juldız belgisi
Start	Басы	Bası
Station	Станция	Stancïya
Statue	Мүсін	Müsin
Stay (sleepover)	Жату, мекендеу	Jatu, mekendew
Steak	Стейк	Steyk
Steal	Ұрлау	Urlaw
Steep	Тік, биік	Tik, bïik
Step	Қадам	Qadam
Stolen	Ұрланған	Urlanğan
Stomach	Қарын	Qarın
Stomach ache	Қарын ауруы	Qarın awruı
Stone	Тас	Tas
Stop (station)	Станция	Stancïya
Stop (halt)	Аялдама	Ayaldama
Stop (avoid)	Доғару	Doğaru
Storm	Дауыл	Dawıl
Story	Оқиға	Oqïğa
Stove	Плита	Plïta
Straight	Тура	Tura
Strange	Біртүрлі	Birtürli
Stranger	Бейтаныс	Beytanıs
Strawberry	Құлпынай	Qulpınay
Street	Көше	Köşe

English	Kazakh	Transliteration
S		
String	Жол	Jol
Stroller	Қаңғыбас	Qañğıbas
Strong	Күшті	Küşti
Stubborn	Қырсық	Qırsıq
Student	Студент	Student
Studio	Студия	Studïya
Stupid	Ақылсыз	Aqılsız
Suburb	Қала маңы	Qala mañı
Subway (underground)	Метро	Metro
Sugar	Қант	Qant
Suitcase	Жол сандық, шабадан	Jol sandıq, şabadan
Summer	Жаз	Jaz
Sun	Күн	Kün
Sun block	Күнқақтылықтан қорғайтын иісмай	Künqaqtılıqtan qorğaytın ïismay
Sunburn	Күнқақтылық	Künqaqtılıq
Sunglasses	Күн көзілдірігі	Kün közildirigi
Sunny	Шуақты	Şuaqtı
Sunrise	Рауан	Rawan
Sunset	Күнбатыс	Künbatıs
Supermarket	Әмбебап дүкені	Ämbebap dükeni
Surf	Соқпа толқын	Soqpa tolqın
Surprise	Тосын	Tosın
Sweater	Свитер	Svïter

English	Kazakh	Transliteration
S		
Sweet	Тәтті	Tätti
Swelling	Ісінгендік	Isingendik
Swim	Жүзу	Jüzu
Swiming pool	Жүзу хауызы	Jüzu xawızı
Swimsuit	Шомылу киімі	Şomılu kïimi
T		
Table	Үстел	Üstel
Tablecloth	Дастархан	Dastarxan
Tall	Ұзын	Uzın
Take	Алу	Alu
Take photos	Фото жасау	Foto jasaw
Talk	Сөйлесу	Söylesu
Tap	Шүмек	Şümek
Tap water	Су құбырының шүмегі	Su qubırınıñ şümegi
Tasty	Дәмді	Dämdi
Tea	Шәй	Şäy
Teacher	Ұстаз	Ustaz
Team	Топ	Top
Teaspoon	Шәй қасық	Şäy qasıq
Teeth	Тістер	Tister
Telephone	Телефон	Telefon
Television	Теледидар	Teledïdar
Tell	Айту	Aytu
Temperature (feverish)	Дене қызуы	Dene qızuı

English	Kazakh	Transliteration
T		
Temperature (degrees)	Температура	Temperatura
Terrible	Қорқынышты	Qorqınıştı
Thank	Рахмет	Raxmet
That (one)	Ол, сол	Ol, sol
Theater	Театр	Teatr
Their	Олардың	Olardıñ
There	Мұнда	Munda
Thermometer	Термометр	Termometr
They	Олар	Olar
Thick	Толық	Tolıq
Thief	Ұры	Urı
Thin	Жіңішке	Jiñişke
Think	Ойлау	Oylaw
Third	Үшінші	Üşinşi
Thirsty (parched)	Шөлдеу	Şöldew
This (one)	Бұл, осы	Bul, osı
Throat	Тамақ	Tamaq
Ticket	Билет	Bïlet
Tight	Тар	Tar
Time	Уақыт	Waqıt
Time difference	Уақыт аралығы	Waqıt aralığı
Tin (aluminium can)	Құты	Qutı
Tiny	Кіп-кішкентай	Kip-kişkentay
Tip (tipping)	Шайпұл	Şaypul

English	Kazakh	Transliteration
T		
Tire	Дөңгелек	Döñgelek
Tired	Шаршау	Şarşaw
Tissues	Маталар	Matalar
To	Арналған	Arnalğan
Toast (toasting)	Тост	Tost
Toaster	Тостер	Toster
Tobacco	Темекі	Temeki
Today	Бүгін	Bügin
Toe	Саусақ	Sawsaq
Together	Бірге	Birge
Toilet	Дәретхана	Däretxana
Toilet paper	Дәретхана қағазы	Däretxana qağazı
Tomato	Қызанақ	Qızanaq
Tomorrow	Ертең	Erteñ
Tonight	Түнде	Tünde
Too (additionally)	-да, -де, -та, -те,	-da, -de, -ta, -te,
Too (excessively)	Тым, аса	Tım, asa
Tooth	Тіс	Tis
Toothbrush	Тіс щёткасы	Tis şçyotkası
Toothpaste	Тіс пастасы	Tis pastası
Touch	Тигізу, қозғау	Tigizu, qozğaw
Tour	Саяхат	Sayaxat
Tourist	Саяхатшы	Sayaxatşı
Towards	Бағытта	Bağıtta

English	Kazakh	Transliteration
T		
Towel	Сүлгі	Sülgi
Tower	Мұнара	Munara
Track (pathway)	Жол	Jol
Track (racing)	Жарыс	Jarıs
Trade (trading)	Сауда-саттық	Sawda-sattıq
Trade (career)	Сатушы	Satuşı
Traffic	Көшедегі көлік қозғалысы	Köşedegi kölik qozğalısı
Traffic light	Бағдаршам	Bağdarşam
Trail	Жол	Jol
Train	Поезд	Poezd
Train station	Вокзал	Vokzal
Tram	Трамвай	Tramvay
Translate	Аудару	Awdaru
Translation	Аударма	Awdarma
Transport	Көлік	Kölik
Travel	Саяхаттау	Sayaxattaw
Tree	Тал	Tal
Trip (expedition)	Сапар	Sapar
Truck	Жүк машинасы	Jük maşïnası
Trust	Сену	Senu
Try (trying)	Тырысу	Tırısu
Try (sip)	Дәмін көру	Dämin köru
T-shirt	Футболка	Futbolka
Turkey	Күркетауық	Kürketawıq

English	Kazakh	Transliteration
T		
Turn	Кезек	Kezek
TV	Теледидар	Teledïdar
Tweezers	Іскек	Iskek
Twice	Екі рет	Eki ret
Twins	Егіздер	Egizder
Two	Екі	Eki
Type	Үлгі	Ülgi
Typical	Үлгіге сәйкес	Ülgige säykes
U		
Umbrella	Қолшатыр	Qolşatır
Uncomfortable	Ыңғайсыз	Iñğaysız
Understand	Түсіну	Tüsinu
Underwear	Ішкиім	Işkïïm
Unfair	Әділетсіз	Ädiletsiz
Until	Дейін	Deyin
Unusual	Әдеттен тыс	Ädetten tıs
Up	Жоғарыға	Joğarığa
Uphill	Тауға	Tawğa
Urgent	Жедел, шұғыл	Jedel, şuğıl
Useful	Пайдалы	Paydalı
V		
Vacation	Демалыс	Demalıs
Valuable	Бағалы	Bağalı
Value	Баға	Bağa

English	Kazakh	Transliteration
V		
Van	Фургон	Furgon
Vegetable	Көкөніс	Kökönis
Vegeterian	Вегетарианшыл	Vegetarïanşıl
Venue	Кездесетін жер	Kezdesetin jer
Very	Өте	Öte
Video recorder	Видеомагнитофон	Vïdeomagnïtofon
View	Көру,қарау	Köru,qaraw
Village	Ауыл	Awıl
Vinegar	Сірке су	Sirke su
Virus	Вирус	Vïrus
Visit	Бару	Baru
Visit	Кіріп шығу, қатынасу	Kirip şığu, qatınasu
Voice	Дауыс	Dawıs
Vote	Дауыс беру	Dawıs beru
W		
Wage	Жалақы	Jalaqı
Wait	Күту	Kütu
Waiter	Даяшы	Dayaşı
Waiting room	Күту залы	Kütu zalı
Wake (someone) up	Ұйқыдан(біреудің) тұруы	Uyqıdan(birewdiñ) turuı
Walk	Серуендеу	Seruendew
Want	Қалау	Qalaw
War	Соғыс	Soğıs
Wardrobe	Гардероб	Garderob

English	Kazakh	Transliteration
V		
Warm	Жылы	Jılı
Warn	Ескерту	Eskertu
Wash (bathe)	Жуыну	Juınu
Wash (scrub)	Тазарту	Tazartu
Wash cloth	Ыдыс-аяқ сүрткіш	Idıs-ayaq sürtkiş
Washing machine	Кір жуатын машина	Kir juatın maşïna
Watch	Сағат	Sağat
Watch	Қарау	Qaraw
Water	Су	Su
Water bottle	Су бөтелкесі	Su bötelkesi
Watermelon	Қарбыз	Qarbız
Waterproof	Су өткізбейтін	Su ötkizbeytin
Wave	Толқын	Tolqın
Way	Жол, тәсіл	Jol, täsil
We	Біз	Biz
Wealthy	Бай	Bay
Wear	Кию	Kïyu
Weather	Ауа райы	Awa rayı
Wedding	Үйлену тойы	Üylenu toyı
Week	Апта	Apta
Weekend	Апта соңы	Apta soñı
Weigh	Ауыр тарту	Awır tartu
Weight	Салмақ	Salmaq
Weights	Гірлер жиынтығы	Girler jïıntığı

English	Kazakh	Transliteration
V		
Welcome	Қош келдіңіздер	Qoş keldiñizder
Well	Жақсы	Jaqsı
West	Батыс	Batıs
Wet	Ылғал, дымқыл	Ilğal, dımqıl
What	Не	Ne
Wheel	Дөңгелек, доңғалақ	Döñgelek, doñğalaq
Wheelchair	Мүгедектер арбашасы	Mügedekter arbaşası
When	Қашан	Qaşan
Where	Қайда	Qayda
Which	Қайсысы	Qaysısı
White	Ақ	Aq
Who	Кім	Kim
Why	Неге	Nege
Wide	Кең	Keñ
Wife	Келіншек	Kelinşek
Win	Жеңу	Jeñu
Wind	Жел	Jel
Window	Терезе	Tereze
Wine	Шарап	Şarap
Winner	Жеңімпаз	Jeñimpaz
Winter	Қыс	Qıs
Wish	Тілеу	Tilew
With	Бірге	Birge
Within (until)	Дейін	Deyin

English	Kazakh	Transliteration
W		
Without	-сыз, -сіз ;	-sız, -siz ;
Wonderful	Керемет	Keremet
Wood	Ағаш	Ağaş
Wool	Жүн	Jün
Word	Сөз	Söz
Work	Жұмыс	Jumıs
World	Ғалам	Ğalam
Worried	Қобалжыған	Qobaljığan
Wrist	Білек	Bilek
Write	Жазу	Jazu
Writer	Жазушы	Jazuşı
Wrong	Бұрыш	Burış
Y		
Year	Жыл	Jıl
Years	Жылдар	Jıldar
Yellow	Сары	Sarı
Yes	Иә	Ïä
Yesterday	Кеше	Keşe
(Not) yet	Әлі (емес)	Äli (emes)
You	Сен	Sen
You	Сіз	Siz
Young	Жас	Jas
Your	Сенің	Seniñ
Z		

English	Kazakh	Transliteration
Z		
Zipper	Сыдырма ілгек	Sıdırma ilgek
Zoo	Хайуанаттар бағы	Xaywanattar bağı
Zucchini	Кәді	Kädi

Kazakh-English Dictionary

Kazakh	Transliteration	English
A		
Автобус	Avtobus	Bus
Автобус аялдамасы	Avtobus ayaldaması	Bus stop
Автовокзал	Avtovokzal	Bus station
Автокөлік	Avtokölik	Car
Ағаш	Ağaş	Wood
Ағаш шебері	Ağaş şeberi	Carpenter
Ағылшын	Ağılşın	English
Адам	Adam	Person
Адамға лық толы	Adamğa lıq tolı	Crowded
Адамдар	Adamdar	People
Адаптер, жалғастырғыш тетік	Adapter, jalğastırğış tetik	Adapter
Аз	Az	Few
Аз	Az	Less
Азық-түлік	Azıq-tülik	Grocery

Kazakh	Transliteration	English
A		
Ай	Ay	Month
Айдау	Aydaw	Go (drive)
Айқай	Ayqay	Shout
Айна	Ayna	Mirror
Айту	Aytu	Say
Айту	Aytu	Tell
Айтылған	Aytılğan	Spoke
Ақ	Aq	White
Ақпарат	Aqparat	Information
Ақша	Aqşa	Money
Ақшыл көк	Aqşıl kök	Blue (light blue)
Ақылсыз	Aqılsız	Stupid
Алақан	Alaqan	Arm
Алаң	Alañ	Square (town center)
Албырт	Albırt	Salmon
Алға, ілгері	Alğa, ilgeri	Ahead
Алғашқы көмек дәрі қорабы	Alğaşqı kömek däri qorabı	First-aid kit
Алдау	Aldaw	Cheat
Алдыңғы күні	Aldıñğı küni	Day before yesterday
Алдында	Aldında	In front of
Алқа	Alqa	Necklace
Алкоголь, есірткіш	Alkogol', esirtkiş	Alcohol
Алкогольсіз сусын	Alkogol'siz susın	Soft-drink
Аллергия	Allergïya	Allergy

Kazakh	Transliteration	English
A		
Алма	Alma	Apple
Алмастыру	Almastıru	Change (pocket change)
Алмұрт	Almurt	Pear
Алтын	Altın	Gold
Алу	Alu	Bring
Алу	Alu	Get
Алу	Alu	Take
Алыс	Alıs	Far
Ана	Ana	Mother
Антиктік, көне	Antïktik, köne	Antique
Апа	Apa	Sister
Апат	Apat	Accident
Апат	Apat	Crash
Апат	Apat	Disaster
Апельсин	Apel'sïn	Orange (citrus)
Апта	Apta	Week
Апта соңы	Apta soñı	Weekend
Арал	Aral	Island
Арасында	Arasında	Between
Арғы күн	Arğı kün	Day after tomorrow
Арзан	Arzan	Cheap
Арқа	Arqa	Back (body)
Арқылы	Arqılı	Across
Арналған	Arnalğan	To

Kazakh	Transliteration	English
A		
Артқы	Artqı	Rear (behind)
Артынан еру	Artınan eru	Follow
Артында	Artında	Back (backward position)
Артында	Artında	Behind
Арыз айту	Arız aytu	Complain
Ас	As	Cook
Ас	As	Meal
Ас бөлмесі	As bölmesi	Kitchen
Асқабақ	Asqabaq	Pumpkin
Аспан	Aspan	Sky
Аспирин	Aspïrïn	Aspirin
Астық, ботқа	Astıq, botqa	Cereal
Астында, төменде	Astında, tömende	Below
Асығу	Asığu	(be) in a hurry
Асықпай	Asıqpay	Slowly
Ат мініп жүру	At minip jüru	Ride (riding)
Ата	Ata	Grandfather
Ата-ана	Ata-ana	Parents
Атақты	Ataqtı	Famous
Атақты	Ataqtı	Popular
Атамұра	Atamura	Relic
Ату	Atu	Shoot
Аты	Atı	Name (term)
Аты-жөні	Atı-jöni	Name (surname)

Kazakh	Transliteration	English
A		
Ауа райы	Awa rayı	Weather
Ауа салқындатқышы	Awa salqındatqışı	Air conditioning
Ауа,әуе	Awa ,äwe	Air
Аударма	Awdarma	Translation
Аудару	Awdaru	Translate
Аурухана	Auruxana	Hospital
Аурухана бөлмесі	Awruxana bölmesi	Room (chamber)
Аурушаң, ауыратын	Auruşañ, auıratın	Painful
Ауыз	Awız	Mouth
Ауыл	Awıl	Village
Ауыр	Auır	Heavy
Ауыр тарту	Awır tartu	Weigh
Ауырғанды басатын	Auırğandı basatın	Painkiller
Ауырту	Auırtu	Hurt
Ауыру	Auıru	Pain
Ауыру, науқас болу	Auıru, nauqas bolu	Ill
Аш	**Aş**	Hungry (famished)
Ашық	Aşıq	Open
Ашық хат	Aşıq xat	Postcard
Ащы	Aşçı	Bitter
Ащы бұрыш	Aşçı burış	Pepper (peppery)
Аяз	Ayaz	Frost
Аяқ	Ayaq	Foot
Аяқ	Ayaq	Leg

Kazakh	Transliteration	English
А		
Аяқ киім	Ayaq kïim	Shoes
Аяқ киімі	Ayaq kïimi	Boots (shoes)
Аялдама	Ayaldama	Stop (halt)
Б		
Баға	Bağa	Cost
Баға	Bağa	Price
Баға	Bağa	Value
Бағалы	Bağalı	Valuable
Бағдар	Bağdar	Route
Бағдарлама	Bağdarlama	Program
Бағдаршам	Bağdarşam	Traffic light
Бағу	Bağu	Care for
Бағыт	Bağıt	Direction
Бағытта	Bağıtta	Towards
Базар, нарық	Bazar, narıq	Market
Бай	Bay	Rich (prosperous)
Бай	Bay	Wealthy
Бақша	Baqşa	Garden
Бақытты	Baqıttı	Happy
Бал	Bal	Honey
Бала	Bala	Baby
Бала	Bala	Child
Бала бақша	Bala baqşa	Kindergarten
Бала күтуші	Bala kütuşi	Babysitter

Kazakh	Transliteration	English
Б		
Балалар	Balalar	Children
Балғын, жаңа	Balğın, jaña	Fresh
Балмұздақ	Balmuzdaq	Ice cream
Балшық	Balşıq	Mud
Балық	Balıq	Fish
Банан	Banan	Banana
Банк	Bank	Bank
Банк шоты	Bank şotı	Bank account
Банкомат	Bankomat	ATM
Бар	Bar	Have
Барлық	Barlıq	All
Бару	Baru	Visit
Бас	Bas	Head
Бас айналу	Bas aynalu	Dizzy
Бас ауыру	Bas auıru	Headache
Бас тарту	Bas tartu	Refuse
Басқа	Basqa	Another
Басқа	Basqa	Other
Басу, итеру	Basu, ïteru	Push
Басшы	Basşı	Chef
Басы	Bası	Start
Батарея	Batareya	Battery
Батыс	Batıs	West
Безе	Beze	Kiss

Kazakh	Transliteration	English
Б		
Бейбітшілік	Beybitşilik	Peace
Бейіт,зират	Beyit,zïrat	Cemetery
Бейтаныс	Beytanıs	Stranger
Бекітулі	Bekituli	Locked
Белгі	Belgi	Sign
Белдемше, юбка	Beldemşe, yubka	Skirt
Бәліш	Bäliş	Pie
Бензин	Benzïn	Petrol
Бері	Beri	Since
Бәрі, барлығы	Bäri, barlığı	Everything
Беру	Beru	Give
Бәс салысу, бәстесу	Bäs salısu, bästesu	Bet
Бәсең	Bäseñ	Slow
Бет	Bet	Page
Бет, жүз	Bet, jüz	Face
Би	Bï	Dance
Билет	Bïlet	Ticket
Билеу	Bïlew	Dancing
Біз	Biz	We
Біздің	Bizdiñ	Our
Білек	Bilek	Wrist
Білім	Bilim	Know
Білім, оқу	Bilim, oqu	Education
Бір	Bir	One

Kazakh	Transliteration	English
Б		
Бір бағытта	Bir bağıtta	One-way
Бір нәрсе	Bir närse	Something
Бір рет	Bir ret	Once
Бір сағат	Bir sağat	Hour
Бірақ	Biraq	But
Бірге	Birge	Together
Бірге	Birge	With
Бірдей	Birdey	Same
Бірдей	Birdey	Similar
Біріктіру	Biriktiru	Make-up
Бірінші	Birinşi	First
Бірнеше	Birneşe	Little (few)
Бірнеше	Birneşe	Several
Біртүрлі	Birtürli	Off (strange)
Біртүрлі	Birtürli	Strange
Біршама	Birşama	Some
Болашақ	Bolaşaq	Future
Болдырмау	Boldırmaw	Cancel
Болу	Bolu	Be
Борт ішінде	Bort işinde	Aboard
Бортқа міну	Bortqa minu	Board (climb aboard)
Бос	Bos	Empty
Босаңсу	Bosañsu	Relax
Босатылу	Bosatılu	Quit

Kazakh	Transliteration	English
Б		
Бөлек	Bölek	Seperate
Бөлік	Bölik	Share (allotment)
Бөлік, тілім	Bölik, tilim	Part (piece)
Бөлшектер	Bölşekter	Details
Бөртпе	Börtpe	Rash
Бөтелке	Bötelke	Bottle
Брондау	Brondaw	Reservation (reserving)
Бүгін	Bügin	Today
Бума, пакет	Buma, paket	Packet
Бұзу	Buzu	Break
Бұзылған	Buzılğan	Spoiled (rotten)
Бұзылған, сынған (сыну)	Buzılğan, sınğan (sınu)	Broken (breaking)
Бұйрық	Buyrıq	Order
Бұл	Bul	It
Бұл, осы	Bul, osı	This (one)
Бұлт	Bult	Cloud
Бұлтты	Bulttı	Cloudy
Бұлшықет	Bulşıqet	Muscle
Бұранда	Buranda	Bottle opener (beer)
Бұрын	Burın	Ago
Бұрын	Burın	Before
Бұрыш	Burış	Corner
Бұрыш	Burış	Wrong

Kazakh	Transliteration	English
В		
Ванна	Vanna	Bath
Вегетарианшыл	Vegetarïanşıl	Vegeterian
Велосипед	Velosïped	Bicycle
Велосипед	Velosïped	Bike
Велосипед айдау	Velosïped aydaw	Cycling
Велосипедші	Velosïpedşi	Cyclist
Видеомагнитофон	Vïdeomagnïtofon	Video recorder
Вирус	Vïrus	Virus
Вокзал	Vokzal	Train station
Г		
Газ	Gaz	Gas (gasoline)
Газет	Gazet	Newspaper
Ғалам	Ğalam	World
Ғаламшар	Ğalamşar	Planet
Ғалым	Ğalım	Scientist
Гардероб	Garderob	Wardrobe
Ғимарат	Ğïmarat	Building
Ғимарат ішінде	Ğïmarat işinde	Indoor
Гитара	Gïtara	Guitar
Гірлер жиынтығы	Girler jïıntığı	Weights
Градустар	Gradustar	Degrees (weather)
Грамм	Gramm	Gram
Гүл	Gül	Flower
Ғылым	Ğılım	Science
Д		
-да, -де, -та, -те,	-da, -de, -ta, -te,	Too (additionally)

Kazakh	Transliteration	English
Д		
Да; де	Da; de	Neither...nor...
-да; -де; -та; -те	-da; -de; -ta; -te	Per
Дабыл, дағыра	Dabıl, dağıra	Drums
Дайвинг	Dayvïng	Diving
Дайын болу	Dayın bolu	Ready
Дайындау	Dayındaw	Prepare
-дан; -ден; -нан; -нен; -тан; -тен;	-dan; -den; -nan; -nen; -tan; -ten;	From
Дастархан	Dastarxan	Tablecloth
Дауыл	Dawıl	Storm
Дауыс	Dawıs	Voice
Дауыс беру	Dawıs beru	Vote
Даяшы	Dayaşı	Waiter
Дезодарант	Dezodarant	Deodorant
Дейін	Deyin	Until
Дейін	Deyin	Within (until)
Дәке	Däke	Gauze
Дәліз, аралық, бөлік	Däliz , aralıq, bölik	Aisle
Демалыс	Demalıs	Rest
Демалыс	Demalıs	Vacation
Демалыс күндері	Demalıs künderi	Holidays
Дәмді	Dämdi	Tasty
Дәмін көру	Dämin köru	Try (sip)
Дәмтатым	Dämtatım	Snack

Kazakh	Transliteration	English
Д		
Дене	Dene	Body
Дене қызуы	Dene qızuı	Temperature (feverish)
Денсаулық	Densawlıq	Health
Депозит	Depozït	Deposit
Дәптерше	Däpterşe	Notebook
Дәретхана	Däretxana	Toilet
Дәретхана қағазы	Däretxana qağazı	Toilet paper
Дәрігер	Däriger	Doctor
Дәріхана	Därixana	Pharmacy
Десерт	Desert	Desert
Джип	Jïp	Jeep
Диета	Dïeta	Diet
Дистанциялық пульт	Dïstancïyalıq pul't	Remote
Дін	Din	Religion
Діни	Dinï	Religious
Доғару	Doğaru	Stop (avoid)
Доп	Dop	Ball (sports)
Дос	Dos	Brother
Дос	Dos	Friend
Дос бала	Dos bala	Boyfriend
Дос қыз	Dos qız	Girlfriend
Дөңгелек	Döñgelek	Round
Дөңгелек	Döñgelek	Tire
Дөңгелек, доңғалақ	Döñgelek, doñğalaq	Wheel

Kazakh	Transliteration	English
Д		
Дүкен	Düken	Shop
Дулыға	Dulığa	Helmet
Дүм, шүйде түбі	Düm, şüyde tübi	Bottom (butt)
Душ, жауын	Duş, jawın	Shower
Дұға оқу	Duğa oqu	Prayer
Е		
Егер	Eger	If
Егеуқұйрық	Egeuquyrıq	Rat
Егіздер	Egizder	Twins
Әдемі	Ädemi	Beautiful
Әдемі	Ädemi	Handsome
Еден	Eden	Floor (carpeting)
Әдеттегідей	Ädettegidey	Ordinary
Әдеттен тыс	Ädetten tıs	Unusual
Әділетсіз	Ädiletsiz	Foul
Әділетсіз	Ädiletsiz	Unfair
Әже	Äje	Grandmother
Ежелгі	Ejelgi	Ancient
Әйел	Äyel	Female
Әке	Äke	Dad
Екі	Eki	Two
Екі рет	Eki ret	Twice
Екінші	Ekinşi	Second
Екіншіден	Ekinşiden	Second (moment)

Kazakh	Transliteration	English
E		
Ел	El	Country
Елге оралу	Elge oralu	Return (homecoming)
Әлдебіреу	Äldebirew	Someone
Әлдеқашан	Äldeqaşan	Already
Әлі (емес)	Äli (emes)	(Not) yet
Әмбебап дүкені	Ämbebap dükeni	Department store
Әмбебап дүкені	Ämbebap dükeni	Supermarket
Емес; -ба; -бе; -ма; -ме; -па; -пе;	Emes; -ba; -be; -ma; -me; -pa; -pe;	Not
Әмиян	Ämïyan	Purse
Ән	Än	Song
Ән айту	Än aytu	Sing
Ең жақын	Eñ jaqın	Nearest
Енгізілген	Engizilgen	Included
Ене	Ene	Mother-in-law
Ену	Enu	Enter
Әнші	Änşi	Singer
Әр	Är	Each
Әр	Är	Every
Ер адам	Er adam	Man
Әрдайым	Ärdayım	Always
Ереже	Ereje	Rule
Ерекше, өзгеше	Erekşe, özgeşe	Rare (unique)
Ересек	Eresek	Adult

Kazakh	Transliteration	English
E		
Ерін	Erin	Lips
Ерін далабы	Erin dalabı	Lipstick
Еріншек	Erinşek	Lazy
Әрқашан	Ärqaşan	Forever
Әркім	Ärkim	Everyone
Еркін	Erkin	Free (at liberty)
Ерте	Erte	Early
Ертең	Erteñ	Tomorrow
Әртіс	Ärtis	Artist
Әртүрлі	Ärtürli	Different
Есеп, шот	Esep, şot	Account
Есептеу	Eseptew	Count
Есік	Esik	Door
Әскери	Äskerï	Military
Ескерту	Eskertu	Warn
Ескі	Eski	Old
Есту	Estu	Hear
Есуас	Esuas	Idiot
Ет	Et	Meat
Әуе компаниясы	Äwe kompanïyası	Airline
Әуежай	Äwejay	Airport
Әуелгі	Äwelgi	Last (previously)
Еуро	Euro	Euro
Ешбір	Eşbir	None

Kazakh	Transliteration	English
E		
Ешқашан	Eşqaşan	Never
Ештеңе	Eşteñe	Nothing
Ж		
Жабу	Jabu	Close
Жабу	Jabu	Shut
Жабық	Jabıq	Closed
Жабысқақ пластырь	Jabısqaq plastır'	Band-Aid
Жаға, жағалау	Jağa, jağalaw	Coast
Жағажай	Jağajay	Beach
Жағдай	Jağday	Shape
Жағу	Jağu	Burn
Жаз	Jaz	Summer
Жазба жұмысы	Jazba jumısı	Paperwork
Жазу	Jazu	Write
Жазушы	Jazuşı	Writer
Жазықсыз, пәк	Jazıqsız, päk	Innocent
Жай, қарапайым	Jay, qarapayım	Simple
Жақ	Jaq	Jaw
Жақсы	Jaqsı	Good
Жақсы	Jaqsı	Well
Жақсы, оң	Jaqsı, oñ	Positive
Жақсы, сүйкімді	Jaqsı, süykimdi	Nice
Жақын	Jaqın	Close (closer)
Жақын	Jaqın	Near (close)

Kazakh	Transliteration	English
Ж		
Жақын арада	Jaqın arada	Soon
Жалақы	Jalaqı	Wage
Жалған ат	Jalğan at	Nickname
Жалғыз	Jalğız	Alone
Жалғыз	Jalğız	Single (individual)
Жалдау	Jaldaw	Rent
Жалықтырғыш	Jalıqtırğış	Boring
Жаман	Jaman	Bad
Жаңа	Jaña	New
Жаңалықтар	Jañalıqtar	News
Жанармай құю станциясы	Janarmay quyu stancïyası	Petrol station
Жанаспалы линзалар	Janaspalı lïnzalar	Contact lenses
Жанаспалы линзалар ерітіндісі	Janaspalı lïnzalar eritindisi	Contact lens solution
Жаңбыр	Jañbır	Rain
Жаңғақ	Jañğaq	Nut
Жануар	Januar	Animal
Жанұя	Januya	Family
Жаны, жағы	Janı, jağı	Side
Жаппай сатылым	Jappay satılım	Sale (special)
Жарақат	Jaraqat	Injury
Жарақат	Jaraqat	Sore
Жарты	Jartı	Half
Жарық	Jarıq	Light
Жарық (бозғылт)	Jarıq (bozğılt)	Light (pale)

Kazakh	Transliteration	English
Ж		
Жарыс	Jarıs	Game (match-up)
Жарыс	Jarıs	Race (running)
Жарыс	Jarıs	Track (racing)
Жас	Jas	Age
Жас	Jas	Young
Жасау	Jasaw	Do
Жасау	Jasaw	Make
Жастық	Jastıq	Pillow
Жастық тысы	Jastıq tısı	Pillowcase
Жасыл	Jasıl	Green
Жату	Jatu	Lie (lying)
Жату, мекендеу	Jatu, mekendew	Stay (sleepover)
Жауап	Jauap	Answer
Жаяу жүруші	Jayaw jürüşi	Pedestrian
Жаяу саяхат	Jayaw sayaxat	Hiking
Жедел	Jedel	Emergency
Жедел, шұғыл	Jedel, şuğıl	Urgent
Жейде, көйлек	Jeyde, köylek	Shirt
Жеке	Jeke	Private
Жел	Jel	Wind
Желім	Jelim	Glue
Жеміс	Jemis	Fruit
Жемпір, тоқыма киім	Jempir, toqıma kïim	Jumper (cardigan)
Және	Jäne	And

Kazakh	Transliteration	English
Ж		
Жеңіл (салмақсыз)	Jeñil (salmaqsız)	Light (weightless)
Жеңімпаз	Jeñimpaz	Winner
Жеңу	Jeñu	Win
Жер	Jer	Land
Жергілікті	Jergilikti	Local
Жержаңғақ	Jerjañğaq	Peanut
Жеткізу	Jetkizu	Deliver
Жеткілікті	Jetkilikti	Enough
Жеу	Jew	Eat
Жиі	Jïi	Often
Жиһаз	Jïhaz	Furniture
Жібек	Jibek	Silk
Жіберу	Jiberu	Send
Жіңішке	Jiñişke	Thin
Жіп	Jip	Rope
Жобалау, ойлау	Jobalaw, oylaw	Guess
Жоғалған	Joğalğan	Lost
Жоғалту	Joğaltu	Lose
Жоғары	Joğarı	Above
Жоғары	Joğarı	High (steep)
Жоғары температура	Joğarı temperatura	Heat
Жоғарыға	Joğarığa	Up
Жоқ	Joq	No
Жол	Jol	Path

Kazakh	Transliteration	English
Ж		
Жол	Jol	Road
Жол	Jol	String
Жол	Jol	Track (pathway)
Жол	Jol	Trail
Жол сандық, шабадан	Jol sandıq, şabadan	Suitcase
Жол, тәсіл	Jol, täsil	Way
Жолаушы	Jolawşı	Passenger
Жорық	Jorıq	Campsite
Жөндеу	Jöndew	Repair
Жөргек	Jörgek	Diaper
Жөтел	Jötel	Cough
Жүгері	Jügeri	Corn
Жүгіріс	Jügiris	Running
Жүгіру	Jügiru	Jogging
Жүгіру	Jügiru	Run
Жүзу	Jüzu	Swim
Жүзу хауызы	Jüzu xawızı	Swiming pool
Жүк	Jük	Baggage
Жүк	Jük	Luggage
Жүк машинасы	Jük maşïnası	Truck
Жүкті алу	Jükti alu	Baggage claim
Жүкті болу	Jükti bolu	Pregnant
Жүн	Jün	Wool
Жүрек	Jürek	Heart

Kazakh	Transliteration	English
Ж		
Жүрек айну	Jürek aynu	Nausea
Журнал	Jurnal	Magazine
Жуынатын бөлме	Juınatın bölme	Bathroom
Жуыну	Juınu	Wash (bathe)
Жұлдыз	Juldız	Star
Жұлдыз белгісі	Juldız belgisi	Star sign
Жұмыртқа	Jumırtqa	Egg
Жұмыс	Jumıs	Job
Жұмыс	Jumıs	Work
Жұмысқа алу	Jumısqa alu	Hire
Жыл	Jıl	Year
Жыл мезгілі	Jıl mezgili	Season
Жылан	Jılan	Snake
Жылдамдық	Jıldamdıq	Speed (rate)
Жылдар	Jıldar	Years
Жылқы	Jılqı	Horse
Жылы	Jılı	Warm
Жылытқыш	Jılıtqış	Heater
Жылыту	Jılıtu	Heated
Жынды	Jındı	Crazy
З		
Заманауи	Zamanauï	Modern
Заң, құқық	Zañ, quqıq	Law (edict)
Заңгер	Zañger	Lawyer

Kazakh	Transliteration	English
3		
Заңды	Zañdı	Legal
Зергерлік бұйымдар	Zergerlik buyımdar	Jewelry
Зират	Zïrat	Grave
И		
Игілікті	Ïgilikti	Grateful
Иә	Ïä	Yes
Иегер	Ïeger	Owner
Иелік қағаз	Ïelik qağaz	Bill (bill of sale)
Иіс	Ïis	Smell
Иісмай	Ïismay	Cream (treatment)
Иіссу	Ïissu	Perfume
Ингредиент	Ïngredïent	Ingredient
Ине	Ïne	Needle (stitch)
Ит	Ït	Dog
Иық	Ïıq	Shoulder
Иыққап, қолдорба	Ïıqqap, qoldorba	Backpack
І		
Іздеу	Izdew	Look for
Ірімшік	Irimşik	Cheese
Ісінгендік	Isingendik	Swelling
Іскек	Iskek	Tweezers
Іш өту	Iş ötu	Diarrhea
Ішімдік	Işimdik	Drink (cocktail)
Ішінара	Işinara	Part-time

Kazakh	Transliteration	English
I		
Ішінде	Işinde	At
Ішінде	Işinde	In
Ішінде	Işinde	Inside
Ішкиім	Işkïim	Underwear
Ішу	Işu	Drink
Қ		
Қабу	Qabu	Bite (dog bite)
Қабырға	Qabırğa	Rib
Қағаз	Qağaz	Paper
Қадақ	Qadaq	Pound (ounces)
Қадам	Qadam	Step
Қажеттілік	Qajettilik	Necessity
Қажеттілік	Qajettilik	Need
Қазір	Qazir	Now
Қайда	Qayda	Where
Қайсысы	Qaysısı	Which
Қайта оралу	Qayta oralu	Return (returning)
Қайта өңдеу	Qayta öñdew	Recycle
Қайтару	Qaytaru	Refund
Қайшы	Qayşı	Scissors
Қайық	Qayıq	Boat
Какао	Kakao	Cocoa
Қақпа	Qaqpa	Gate (airport)
Қала	Qala	City

Kazakh	Transliteration	English
Қ		
Қала маңы	Qala mañı	Suburb
Қала орталығы	Qala ortalığı	City center
Қалай	Qalay	How
Қалам	Qalam	Pen
Қаламсап	Qalamsap	Pencil
Қалау	Qalaw	Prefer
Қалау	Qalaw	Want
Қалжың, әзіл	Qaljıñ, äzil	Joke
Қалпақ	Qalpaq	Hat
Қалта	Qalta	Pocket
Қалыңдық	Qalıñdıq	Bribe
Камера	Kamera	Camera
Қан	Qan	Blood
Қаңғыбас	Qañğıbas	Stroller
Қант	Qant	Sugar
Қанша	Qanşa	How much
Қаңылтыр құты	Qañıltır qutı	Can (aluminium can)
Қаптама	Qaptama	Package
Қар	Qar	Snow
Қара	Qara	Black
Қараңғы	Qarañğı	Dark
Қарау	Qaraw	Look
Қарау	Qaraw	Watch
Қарбыз	Qarbız	Watermelon

Kazakh	Transliteration	English
Қ		
Қарсы	Qarsı	Opposite
Карта	Karta	Map
Картоп	Kartop	Potato
Қару, мылтық	Qaru, mıltıq	Gun
Қарызға алу	Qarızğa alu	Borrow
Қарым-қатынас	Qarım-qatınas	Relationship
Қарын	Qarın	Stomach
Қарын ауруы	Qarın awruı	Stomach ache
Кассир	Kassir	Cashier
Қасық	Qasıq	Spoon
Қасында, жақын	Qasında, jaqın	Next to
Қасында, жанында	Qasında, janında	Beside
Қатар	Qatar	Floor (level)
Қате	Qate	Bug
Қателік	Qatelik	Mistake
Қатты	Qattı	Hard (firm)
Қатты қайнатылған, пісірілген	Qattı qaynatılğan, pisirilgen	Hard-boiled
Қауіпсіз	Qawipsiz	Safe
Қауіпсіздік белдемшесі	Qawipsizdik beldemşesi	Seatbelt
Қауіпті	Qauipti	Dangerous
Кафедралы собор	Kafedralı sobor	Cathedral
Қашан	Qaşan	When
Кедей	Kedey	Poor
Кедейлік	Kedeylik	Poverty

Kazakh	Transliteration	English
Қ		
Кеден	Keden	Customs
Кәді	Kädi	Zucchini
Кездесетін жер	Kezdesetin jer	Venue
Кездесу	Kezdesu	Date (companion)
Кездесу	Kezdesu	Meet
Кездесу	Kezdesu	Meeting
Кездесу, тағайындау	Kezdesu, tağayındau	Appointment
Кезек	Kezek	Queue
Кезек	Kezek	Turn
Кейін	Keyin	After
Келесі	Kelesi	Next (ensuing)
Келіншек	Kelinşek	Wife
Келісім	Kelisim	Deal (card dealer)
Келісімшарт	Kelisimşart	Contract
Келісу	Kelisu	Agree
Келу	Kelu	Arrive
Келу	Kelu	Come
Келуі	Kelui	Arrivals
Кеме	Keme	Ship
Кемежай	Kemejay	Port (dock)
Кәмпит	Kämpït	Candy
Кең	Keñ	Wide
Кеңес	Keñes	Advice
Кеңсе	Keñse	Office

Kazakh	Transliteration	English
Қ		
Кепілді	Kepildi	Guaranteed
Кептіру	Keptiru	Dry (warm up)
Керемет	Keremet	Wonderful
Керең, саңырау	Kereñ, sañıraw	Deaf
Кереует	Kerewet	Bed
Керу	Keru	Cross (crucifix)
Кәсіп	Käsip	Business
Кәсіпорын	Käsiporın	Shop
Кәстрөл	Käström	Pan
Кәстрөл	Käström	Saucepan
Кету, артқа басу	Ketu, artqa basu	Depart
Кеуде, төс	Keude, tös	Chest (torso)
Кеш	Keş	Evening
Кеше	Keşe	Yesterday
Киім ауыстыратын орын	Kïim awıstıratın orın	Changin room
Киім дүкені	Kïim dükeni	Clothing store
Киіну	Kïinu	Clothing
Килограмм	Kїlogramm	Kilogram
Кино	Kïno	Movie
Қираған үйінді	Qïrağan üyindi	Ruins
Қиын	Qïın	Difficult
Кию	Kïyu	Wear
Қию	Qïyu	Cut
Кідіріс, тұрып қалу	Kidiris, turıp qalu	Delay

Kazakh	Transliteration	English
Қ		
Кілем	Kilem	Rug
Кілт	Kilt	Key
Кім	Kim	Who
Кінәлі	Kinäli	Guilty
Кіп-кішкентай	Kip-kişkentay	Little (tiny)
Кіп-кішкентай	Kip-kişkentay	Tiny
Кір жуатын машина	Kir juatın maşïna	Washing machine
Кіріп шығу, қатынасу	Kirip şığu, qatınasu	Visit
Кіріс, пайда	Kiris, payda	Profit
Кіру	Kiru	Entry
Кітап	Kitap	Book
Кітап дукені	Kitap dükeni	Bookshop
Кітапхана	Kitapxana	Library
Кішкентай	Kişkentay	Small
Кішкентай шам	Kişkentay şam	Light bulb
Қобалжыған	Qobaljığan	Worried
Қоғамдық дәретхана	Qoğamdıq däretxana	Public toilet
Коктейль	Kokteyl'	Cocktail
Қоқыс	Qoqıs	Garbage
Қоқыс шелегі	Qoqıs şelegi	Garbage can
Қол	Qol	Hand
Қол қойылу	Qol qoyılu	Signature
Қол қою	Qol qoyu	Sign (signature)
Қол орамал	Qol oramal	Handkerchief

Kazakh	Transliteration	English
Қ		
Қол тимеу	Qol tïmew	Busy
Қолбасшы	Qolbasşı	Leader
Қолғап	Qolğap	Gloves
Қолдан жасалған	Qoldan jasalğan	Handmade
Қолдан келу, жасай алу	Qoldan kelu, jasay alu	Can (have the ability)
Қолдорба	Qoldorba	Handbag
Колледж	Kolledj	College
Қолма-қол төлеу	Qolma-qol tölew	Cash
Қолөнер	Qolöner	Crafts
Қолшатыр	Qolşatır	Umbrella
Компасс	Kompass	Compass
Компьютер	Kompyuter	Computer
Қонақ үй	Qonaq üy	Hotel
Қонақ үй	Qonaq üy	Motel
Қонақүй нөмірі	Qonaqüy nömiri	Room (accommodation)
Кондиционер (шашқа арналған)	Kondïcïoner (şaşqa arnalğan)	Conditioner (conditioning treatment)
Концерт	Koncert	Concert
Қоңыр	Qoñır	Brown
Қоңырау	Qoñıraw	Ring (ringing)
Қорап	Qorap	Box
Қорған	Qorğan	Castle
Қорғау	Qorğaw	Protect
Қоржын	Qorjın	Basket

Kazakh	Transliteration	English
Қ		
Қорқу, қорыққан	Qorqu, qorıqqan	Afraid
Қорқыныш	Qorqınış	Fare
Қорқынышты	Qorqınıştı	Awful
Қорқынышты	Qorqınıştı	Terrible
Қос	Qos	Double
Қос бөлме	Qos bölme	Double room
Қос кереует	Qos kerewet	Double bed
Қос, екеуі де	Qos, ekewi de	Both
Қос, жұп	Qos, jup	Pair
Кофе	Kofe	Coffee
Қош келдіңіздер	Qoş keldiñizder	Welcome
Қоян	Qoyan	Rabbit
Көбелек	Köbelek	Butterfly
Көбірек	Köbirek	More
Көгершін	Kögerşin	Pigeon
Көздер	Közder	Eyes
Көзілдірік	Közildirik	Glasses (eyeglasses)
Көйлек	Köylek	Dress
Көк	Kök	Blue (dark blue)
Көкөніс	Kökönis	Vegetable
Көктем	Köktem	Spring (prime)
Көлеңке	Köleñke	Shade (shady)
Көлік	Kölik	Transport
Көлік жүргізу, айдау	Kölik jürgizu, aydaw	Drive

Kazakh	Transliteration	English
Қ		
Көмек	Kömek	Help
Көңіл көтеру	Köñil köteru	Have fun
Көңілді	Köñildi	Funny
Көңілсіз	Köñilsiz	Sad
Көп	Köp	Lot
Көп,көптеген	Köp,köptegen	Many
Көпір	Köpir	Bridge
Көрініс	Körinis	Performance
Көрме	Körme	Show
Көрпе	Körpe	Blanket
Көрсету	Körsetu	Show
Көру	Köru	See
Көру,қарау	Köru,qaraw	View
Көтерілу	Köterilu	Climb
Көше	Köşe	Street
Көшедегі көлік қозғалысы	Köşedegi kölik qozğalısı	Traffic
Крем	Krem	Cream (creamy)
Круиз	Kruïz	Cruise
Қуаттылық, күш	Quattılıq, küş	Power
Куәландыру картасы	Kuälandıru kartası	ID card
Куәлік	Kuälik	Identification
Күз	Küz	Fall (autumnal)
Күйеу	Küyew	Husband
Күйіктас	Küyiktas	Pottery

Kazakh	Transliteration	English
Қ		
Күлімсіреу	Külimsirew	Smile
Күміс	Kümis	Silver
Күн	Kün	Date (important notice)
Күн	Kün	Date (specific day)
Күн	Kün	Day
Күн	Kün	Sun
Күн көзілдірігі	Kün közildirigi	Sunglasses
Күнбатыс	Künbatıs	Sunset
Күнделік	Kündelik	Diary
Күнделікті	Kündelikti	Daily
Күнқақтылық	Künqaqtılıq	Sunburn
Күнқақтылықтан қорғайтын иісмай	Künqaqtılıqtan qorğaytın ïismay	Sun block
Күріш	Küriş	Rice
Күркетауық	Kürketawıq	Turkey
Күрте	Kürte	Jacket
Күту	Kütu	Wait
Күту залы	Kütu zalı	Waiting room
Күшті	Küşti	Strong
Күшті, қатты	Küşti, qattı	Loud
Қуыру	Quıru	Fry
Құдай	Quday	God (deity)
Құқық	Quqıq	Right (appropriate)
Құлақ	Qulaq	Ear

Kazakh	Transliteration	English
Қ		
Құлау	Qulaw	Fall (falling)
Құлпынай	Qulpınay	Strawberry
Құлып	Qulıp	Lock
Құлып	Qulıp	Padlock
Құм	Qum	Sand
Құрғақ	Qurğaq	Dry
Құру	Quru	Build
Құрылысшы	Qurılısşı	Builder
Құс	Qus	Bird
Құты	Qutı	Tin (aluminium can)
Құшақ	Quşaq	Hug
Қыз	Qız	Girl
Қызанақ	Qızanaq	Tomato
Қызғылт	Qızğılt	Pink
Қызғылт сары	Qızğılt sarı	Orange (color)
Қызмет көрсету	Qızmet körsetu	Service
Қызу	Qızu	Fever
Қызы	Qızı	Daughter
Қызық	Qızıq	Fun
Қызықтау	Qızıqtaw	Enjoy (enjoying)
Қызықты	Qızıqtı	Interesting
Қызыл	Qızıl	Red
Қызылкүрең	Qızılküreñ	Purple
Қымбат	Qımbat	Expensive

Kazakh	Transliteration	English
Қ		
Қырсық	Qırsıq	Stubborn
Қыру, қырыну	Qıru, qırınu	Shave
Қырынуға арналған иісмай	Qırınuğa arnalğan iismay	Shaving cream
Қыс	Qıs	Winter
Қысқа	Qısqa	Short (low)
Қысқа толқынды пеш	Qısqa tolqındı peş	Microwave
Қысым	Qısım	Pressure
Қыша	Qışa	Mustard
Қышу	Qışu	Itch
Л		
Лагерь	Lager'	Camp
Лайм	Laym	Lime
Лақап ат	Laqap at	Name (moniker)
Лас	Las	Dirty
Ластану	Lastanu	Pollution
Лесбияндық	Lesbïyandıq	Lesbian
Ликёрлі-арақ зауыты	Lïkyorli-araq zauıtı	Liquor store
Лимон	Lïmon	Lemon
Лимонад	Lïmonad	Lemonade
М		
Май	May	Butter
Май (майлы)	May (maylı)	Oil (oily)
Майлық	Maylıq	Napkin
Майшам	Mayşam	Candle

Kazakh	Transliteration	English
М		
Мақта	Maqta	Cotton
Мақта дөңгелектері	Maqta döñgelekteri	Cotton balls
Маман	Maman	Specialist
Маңызды	Mañızdı	Important
Марка	Marka	Stamp
Мас	Mas	Drunk
Маса	Masa	Mosquito
Маталар	Matalar	Tissues
Матрас	Matras	Mattress
Махаббат	Maxabbat	Love
Машина	Maşïna	Machine
Медицина	Medïcïna	Medicine (medicinals)
Мейірбике	Meyirbïke	Nurse
Мейрамхана	Meyramxana	Restaurant
Мекенжай	Mekenjay	Address
Мектеп	Mektep	School
Мемлекет	Memleket	Government
Мен	Men	Me
Менің	Meniñ	My
Мереке	Mereke	Holiday
Мерекелеу, тойлау	Merekelew, toylaw	Celebration
Металл	Metall	Metal
Метр	Metr	Meter
Метро	Metro	Subway (underground)

Kazakh	Transliteration	English
M		
Миллиметр	Millimetr	Millimeter
Минут	Minut	Minute (moment)
Мінсіз	Minsiz	Perfect
Мойын	Moyın	Neck
Мойындау, кіру	Moyındau, kiru	Admit
Мойынорағыш	Moyınorağış	Scarf
Молда	Molda	Priest
Молшылық, байлық	Molşılıq, baylıq	Luxury
Монша	Monşa	Sauna
Моторлы қайық	Motorlı qayıq	Motorboat
Мотоцикл	Motocīkl	Motorbike
Мүгедектер арбашасы	Mügedekter arbaşası	Wheelchair
Музыка	Muzıka	Music
Музыка жазу	Muzıka jazu	Record (music)
Мүмкін болу	Mümkin bolu	Can (allowed)
Мүмкін болу	Mümkin bolu	Maybe
Мүмкін болу	Mümkin bolu	Possible
Мүмкін емес	Mümkin emes	Impossible
Мүмкіндік	Mümkindik	Chance
Мүсін	Müsin	Statue
Мүше	Müşe	Member
Мұз	Muz	Ice
Мұнара	Munara	Tower
Мұнда	Munda	Here

Kazakh	Transliteration	English
M		
Мұнда	Munda	There
Мұражай	Murajay	Museum
Мұрын	Murın	Nose
Мұхит	Muxït	Ocean
Мылқау	Mılqaw	Mute
Мырза	Mırza	Kind (sweet)
Мырза	Mırza	Mr.
Мысық	Mısıq	Cat
Н		
Нақты	Naqtı	Exactly
Нан	Nan	Bread
Нан дүкені	Nan dükeni	Bakery
Науқас	Nawqas	Sick
Не	Ne	What
Неге	Nege	Why
Негізгі	Negizgi	Main
Негізгі жол	Negizgi jol	Mainroad
Немере қыз	Nemere qız	Granddaughter
Немере ұл	Nemere ul	Grandson
Немесе	Nemese	Or
Несие	Nesïe	Credit
Несие картасы	Nesïe kartası	Credit card
Ноутбук	Noutbuk	Laptop
Нөмір	Nömir	Number

Kazakh	Transliteration	English
Н		
Нөмір саны	Nömir sanı	Room number
Нүкте	Nükte	Point
О		
Обьектив	Ob'ektïv	Lens
Ойлау	Oylaw	Think
ойнау	oynaw	Pay
Ойнау, тарту	Oynaw, tartu	Play (strum)
Ойын картасы	Oyın kartası	Cards (playing cards)
Ойын-сауық	Oyin-sawıq	Game (event)
Оқиға	Oqïğa	Story
Оқу	Oqu	Read
Оқу	Oqu	Reading
Ол	**Оl**	He
Ол	**Оl**	She
Ол, сол	**Оl, sol**	That (one)
Олар	Olar	They
Олардың	Olardıñ	Their
Оңай, жеңіл	Oñay, jeñil	Easy
Оңға	Oñğa	Right (rightward)
Оңтүстік	Oñtüstik	South
Оның	Onıñ	His
Оның, онікі	Onıñ, oniki	Her (hers)
Оператор	Operator	Operator
Операция	Operacïya	Operation (process)

Kazakh	Transliteration	English
О		
Орамал	Oramal	Bandage
Оркестр	Orkestr	Orchestra
Орман	Orman	Forest
Орта мектеп	Orta mektep	High school
Орталық	Ortalıq	Center
Орын	Orın	Place
Орындық	Orındıq	Chair
Орындық	Orındıq	Seat
Осы шақ	Osı şaq	Present (now)
От, алауошақ	**Ot,** alawoşaq	Fire (heated)
Оттегі	Ottegi	Oxygen
Оттық, шақпақ	Ottıq, şaqpaq	Lighter (ignited)
Отын	Otın	Campfire
Отырғызу талоны	Otırğızu talonı	Boarding pass
Отыру	Otıru	Sit
Оятқыш	Oyatqış	Alarm clock
Ө		
Өжет	Öjet	Brave
Өзгеріс	Özgeris	Change
Өзен	Özen	Lake
Өзен	Özen	River
Өзімшіл	Özimşil	Selfish
Өйткені	Öytkeni	Because
Өкіну	Ökinu	Regret

Kazakh	Transliteration	English
Ө		
Өлген	Ölgen	Dead
Өлтіру	Öltiru	Murder
Өлу, қайтып қалу	Ölu, qaytıp qalu	Die
Өлшем	Ölşem	Size (extent)
Өмір	Ömir	Life
Өмір сүру	Ömir süru	Live (occupy)
Өндіру	Öndiru	Produce
Өнер	Öner	Art
Өрік	Örik	Plum
Өсімдік	Ösimdik	Plant
Өсу	Ösu	Grow
Өте	**Ö**te	Very
Өте жақсы	Öte jaqsı	Best
Өтірік айту	Ötirik aytu	Lie (falsehood)
Өтірікші	Ötirikşi	Liar
Өткен	Ötken	Past (ago)
Өшірілген, сөнген	Öşirilgen, söngen	Disabled
П		
Паб	Pab	Pub
Пайдалы	Paydalı	Useful
Пайыз	Payız	Per cent
Пансионда тұрушы	Pansïonda turuşı	Border
Парасатты, ақылды	Parasattı, aqıldı	Sensible
Паркинг	Parkïng	Park (parking)

Kazakh	Transliteration	English
П		
Партия	Partïya	Party (political)
Паспорт	Pasport	Passport
Патша	Patşa	King
Патшайым	Patşayım	Queen
Педаль	Pedal'	Pedal
Пәлте	Pälte	Coat
Пернетақта	Pernetaqta	Keyboard
Пәтер	Päter	Apartment
Пәтер	Päter	Flat
Печенье	Peçen'e	Cookie
Пеш	Peş	Oven
Пікір	Pikir	Opinion
Пікірталасу	Pikirtalasu	Argue
Пластик	Plastïk	Plastic
Плащ	Plaşç	Raincoat
Плита	Plïta	Stove
Поезд	Poezd	Train
Полицей	Polïcey	Police
Полиция бөлімі	Polïcïya bölimi	Police station
Полиция офицері	Polïcïya ofïceri	Police officer
Пошта (пошталық)	Poşta (poştalıq)	Mail (mailing)
Пошта бөлімі	Poşta bölimi	Post office
Пошта жәшігі	Poşta jäşigi	Mailbox
Президент, елбасы	Prezïdent, elbası	President

Kazakh	Transliteration	English
П		
Принтер	Prïnter	Printer (printing)
Пышақ	Pışaq	Knife
Пьеса	P'esa	Play (theatrical)
Р		
Радиатор	Radïator	Radiator
Радио	Radïo	Radio
Рауан	Rawan	Sunrise
Рахмет	Raxmet	Thank
Рецепт	Recept	Prescription
Рождество	Rojdestvo	Christmas
Рок, жазмыш	Rok, jazmış	Rock
Ром	Rom	Rum
Романтикалық	Romantïkalıq	Romantic
Рұқсат	Ruqsat	Permission (permit)
С		
Сабын	Sabın	Soap
Сағат	Sağat	Clock
Сағат	Sağat	Watch
Сағынған, іші пысқан	Sağınğan, işi pısqan	Bored
Сақина	Saqïna	Ring (bauble)
Салат	Salat	Lettuce
Салат	Salat	Salad
Салқын	Salqın	Cool (mild temperature)
Салмақ	Salmaq	Weight

Kazakh	Transliteration	English
С		
Салмақты	Salmaqtı	Serious
Салт-дәстүр	Salt-dästür	Custom
Салу, қою	Salu, qoyu	Put
Сандал	Sandal	Sandal
Сантиметр	Santïmetr	Centimeter
Сапа	Sapa	Quality
Сапар	Sapar	Ride
Сапар	Sapar	Trip (expedition)
Сары	Sarı	Yellow
Сату	Satu	Sell
Сатушы	Satuşı	Trade (career)
Сатылым салығы	Satılım salığı	Sales tax
Сатып алу	Satıp alu	Buy
Сауал	Sawal	Ask (request)
Сауда орталығы	Sawda ortalığı	Shopping center
Сауда-саттық	Sawda-sattıq	Trade (trading)
Саумалдық	Sawmaldıq	Spinach
Саусақ	Sausaq	Finger
Саусақ	Sawsaq	Toe
Саябақ	Sayabaq	Park
Саясат	Sayasat	Politics
Саяхат	Sayaxat	Hike
Саяхат	Sayaxat	Tour
Саяхаттау	Sayaxattaw	Travel

Kazakh	Transliteration	English
С		
Саяхатшы	Sayaxatşı	Tourist
Свитер	Svïter	Sweater
Себеп	Sebep	Reason
Сәбіз	Säbiz	Carrot
Сезімдер	Sezimder	Feelings
Сезімтал	Sezimtal	Sensual
Сезу	Sezu	Feel (touching)
Секілді, ұқсас	Sekildi, uqsas	Like
Секс	Seks	Sex
Сексизм	Seksïzm	Sexism
Сексуалды	Seksualdı	Sexy
Семіз	Semiz	Fat
Сен	Sen	You
Сең, үйінді	Señ, üyindi	Lump
Сенің	Seniñ	Your
Сену	Senu	Trust
Серуендеу	Seruendew	Go (walk)
Серуендеу	Seruendew	Walk
Сәтсіздік	Sätsizdik	Miss (mishap)
Сәтті	Sätti	Lucky
Сәттілік	Sättilik	Luck
Сигара	Sïgara	Cigar
Сидр	Sïdr	Cider
Сирек кездесетін	Sïrek kezdesetin	Rare (exotic)

Kazakh	Transliteration	English
C		
Сиыр	Sïır	Cow
Сиыр еті	Sïır eti	Beef
Сіз	Siz	You
Сіңір созылуы	Siñir sozıluı	Sprain
Сіріңке	Siriñke	Matches (matchbox)
Сірке су	Sirke su	Vinegar
Соғыс	Soğıs	War
Содалы су	Sodalı su	Soda
Соқпа толқын	Soqpa tolqın	Surf
Соқыр	Soqır	Blind
Сол сияқты	Sol sïyaqtı	Also
Сол, сол жақ	Sol, sol jaq	Left (leftward)
Солтүстік	Soltüstik	North
Соңғы	Soñğı	Last (finale)
Соңғы уақытта	Soñğı waqıtta	Recently
Соңы	Soñı	End
Сорғыш	Sorğış	Pump
Сорпа, көже	Sorpa, köje	Soup
Сөз	Söz	Word
Сөз беру	Söz beru	Promise
Сөйлесу	Söylesu	Chat up
Сөйлесу	Söylesu	Talk
Сөмке	Sömke	Bag
Спорт залы	Sport zalı	Gym

Kazakh	Transliteration	English
C		
Стадион	Stadïon	Stadium
Стақан	Staqan	Glass
Станция	Stancïya	Station
Станция	Stancïya	Stop (station)
Стейк	Steyk	Steak
Студент	Student	Student
Студия	Studïya	Studio
Су	Su	Water
Су бөтелкесі	Su bötelkesi	Water bottle
Су құбырының шүмегі	Su qubırınıñ şümegi	Tap water
Су өткізбейтін	Su ötkizbeytin	Waterproof
Сүйкімді	Süykimdi	Pretty
Сүлгі	Sülgi	Towel
Сурет	Suret	Painting (canvas)
Сурет өнері	Suret öneri	Painting (the art)
Суретші	Suretşi	Painter
Сүрсүбе	Sürsübe	Bacon
Сусабын	Susabın	Shampoo
Сусын	Susın	Drink (beverage)
Сүт	Süt	Milk
Суық	Suıq	Cold
Суық тию	Suıq tïyu	Have a cold
Сүю	Süyu	Kiss
Сұрақ	Suraq	Question

Kazakh	Transliteration	English
С		
Сұрау	Surau	Ask (questinoning)
Сұры	Surı	Grey
Сыдырма ілгек	Sıdırma ilgek	Zipper
-сыз, -сіз ;	-sız, -siz ;	Without
Сыйлық	Sıylıq	Gift
Сыйлық	Sıylıq	Present (treat)
Сынғыш	Sınğış	Fragile
Сыра	Sıra	Beer
Сыртқа	Sırtqa	Outside
Т		
Таба	Taba	Frying pan
Табиғат	Tabïğat	Nature
Таблетка	Tabletka	Pill
Табыс табу	Tabıs tabu	Earn
Таза	Taza	Clean
Таза, қоспасыз	Taza, qospasız	Pure
Тазалау	Tazalaw	Cleaning
Тазарту	Tazartu	Wash (scrub)
Тал	Tal	Tree
Тамақ	Tamaq	Food
Тамақ	Tamaq	Throat
Тамаша	Tamaşa	Fine
Таң	Tañ	Morning
Таң ату, басы	Tañ atu, bası	Dawn

Kazakh	Transliteration	English
T		
Таңғы ас	Tañğı as	Breakfast
Таңдау	Tañdaw	Choose
Таңқурай	Tañquray	Raspberry
Тапсыру	Tapsıru	Pass
Тапсырыс	Tapsırıs	Order
Тапшылық	Tapşılıq	Shortage
Тар	Tar	Tight
Тарақ	Taraq	Comb
Тарақ	Taraq	Hairbrush
Тарақан	Taraqan	Cockroach
Тарих	Tarïx	History
Тарту	Tartu	Pull
Тас	Tas	Stone
Тас жол	Tas jol	Highway
Тасу	Tasu	Carry
Тасымалдау	Tasımaldaw	Carriage
Тау	Taw	Mountain
Тау жотасы	Taw jotası	Mountain range
Тауға	Tawğa	Uphill
Тауық еті	Tawıq eti	Chicken
Театр	Teatr	Theater
Тегін	Tegin	Complimentary (on the house)
Тегін	Tegin	Free (no cost)
Тәжірибе	Täjirïbe	Experience

Kazakh	Transliteration	English
T		
Тез, жылдам	Tez, jıldam	Fast
Тез, лезде	Tez, lezde	Quick
Тек қана	Tek qana	Only
Теледидар	Teledïdar	Television
Теледидар	Teledïdar	TV
Телефон	Telefon	Cell phone
Телефон	Telefon	Telephone
Телефон кітапшасы	Telefon kitapşası	Phone book
Телефон шалу	Telefon şalu	Call (telephone call)
Темекі	Temeki	Tobacco
Температура	Temperatura	Temperature (degrees)
Теңіз	Teñiz	Sea
Теңіз ауруы	Teñiz awruı	Seasickness
Терезе	Tereze	Window
Тәрелке	Tärelke	Plate
Терең	Tereñ	Deep
Тері	Teri	Leather
Тері	Teri	Skin
Теріс, жағымғыз	Teris, jağımğız	Negative
Термометр	Termometr	Thermometer
Тәтті	Tätti	Sweet
Тигізу, қозғау	Tïgizu, qozğaw	Touch
Тиындар	Tïındar	Coins
Тігу	Tïgu	Sew

Kazakh	Transliteration	English
T		
Тізе	Tize	Knee
Тік, биік	Tik, biik	Steep
Тіл	Til	Language
Тілеу	Tilew	Wish
Тілім, бөлік	Tilim, bölik	Piece
Тілім, үзім	Tilim, üzim	Slice
Тіс	Tis	Tooth
Тіс дәрігері	Tis därigeri	Dentist
Тіс пастасы	Tis pastası	Toothpaste
Тіс щёткасы	Tis şçyotkası	Toothbrush
Тістер	Tister	Teeth
Тобық	Tobıq	Ankle
Той	Toy	Party (celebration)
Той торты	Toy tortı	Cake (wedding cake)
Тоқтау	Toqtaw	Finish
Толқын	Tolqın	Wave
Толтыру	Toltıru	Fill
Толы	Tolı	Full
Толық	Tolıq	Thick
Толық қамтылу	Tolıq qamtılu	Full-time
Тоңазытқыш	Toñazıtqış	Fridge
Тоңазытқыш	Toñazıtqış	Refrigerator
Тонау	Tonaw	Rob
Тонау, алаяқтық	Tonaw, alayaqtıq	Rip-off

Kazakh	Transliteration	English
T		
Тонаушылық	Tonawşılıq	Robbery
Топ	Top	Class (categorize)
Топ	Top	Team
Топ (музыкалық)	Top (muzıkalıq)	Band (musician)
Тор, желі	Tor, jeli	Net
Тост	Tost	Toast (toasting)
Тостер	Toster	Toaster
Тосын	Tosın	Surprise
Төбе	Töbe	Hill
Төбелесу	Töbelesu	Fight
Төлем	Tölem	Payment
Төлеу	Tölew	Cash (deposit a check)
Төмен	Tömen	Down
Төмен	Tömen	Low
Төсек жайма	Tösek jayma	Sheet (linens)
Трамвай	Tramvay	Tram
Түбінде	Tübinde	Bottom (on bottom)
Түбіртек	Tübirtek	Receipt
Туған күн	Tuğan kün	Birthday
Туған күнге арналған торт	Tuğan künge arnalğan tort	Cake (birthday cake)
Түн	Tün	Night
Түн ортасы	Tün ortası	Midnight
Түнгі клуб	Tüngi klub	Nightclub
Түнде	Tünde	Tonight

Kazakh	Transliteration	English
T		
Түні бойы	Tüni boyı	Overnight
Түпкі	Tüpki	Original
Тура	Tura	Direct
Тура	Tura	Straight
Туралы, жөнінде	Turalı, jöninde	About
Түрме	Türme	Jail
Түрме	Türme	Prison
Түс	Tüs	Color
Түс кезі	Tüs kezi	Midday
Түс кезі	Tüs kezi	Noon
Түс, арман	Tüs, arman	Dream
Түсіну	Tüsinu	Understand
Түскі ас	Tüski as	Dinner
Түскі ас	Tüski as	Lunch
Түсу, түсіру	Tüsu, tüsiru	Downhill
Түтін	Tütin	Smoke
Тұз	Tuz	Salt
Тұздық	Tuzdıq	Sauce
Тұман	Tuman	Foggy
Тұрмыс құру	Turmıs quru	Marriage
Тұтқындау	Tutqındau	Arrest
Тығын	Tığın	Plug (stopper)
Тым, аса	Tım, asa	Too (excessively)
Тыңдау	Tıñdaw	Listen

Kazakh	Transliteration	English
Т		
Тыныс	Tınıs	Breathe
Тыныш	Tınış	Quiet
Тырнақ тістеуігі	Tırnaq tistewigi	Nail clippers
Тырысу	Tırısu	Try (trying)
Тышқан	Tışqan	Mouse
У		
Уақыт	Waqıt	Time
Уақыт аралығы	Waqıt aralığı	Time difference
Уақытында	Waqıtında	On time
Ү		
Үй	**Üy**	Home
Үй	**Üy**	House
Үйден шығу	Üyden şığu	Go out
Үйлену	Üylenu	Marry
Үйлену тойы	Üylenu toyı	Wedding
Үйрек	Üyrek	Duck
Үйрену	Üyrenu	Learn
Үлгі	Ülgi	Type
Үлгіге сәйкес	Ülgige säykes	Typical
Үлес	Üles	Share (sharing)
Үлкен	Ülken	Big
Үлкен	Ülken	Large
Улы	Ulı	Poisonous
Үстел	Üstel	Table

Kazakh	Transliteration	English
Y		
Үстінде	Üstinde	On
Үшінші	Üşinşi	Third
Ұ		
Ұзын	Uzın	Long
Ұзын	Uzın	Tall
Ұйқыдан(біреудің) тұруы	Uyqıdan(birewdiñ) turuı	Wake (someone) up
Ұйқылы	Uyqılı	Sleepy
Ұйықтайтын бөлме	Uyıqtaytın bölme	Bedroom
Ұйықтау	Uyıqtaw	Sleep
Ұл	Ul	Boy
Ұл	Ul	Son
Ұлы	Ulı	Great (wonderful)
Ұмыту	Umıtu	Forget
Ұн	Un	Flour
Ұнтақ	Untaq	Powder
Ұрланған	Urlanğan	Stolen
Ұрлау	Urlaw	Steal
Ұры	Urı	Thief
Ұсақтау	Usaqtaw	Change (coinage)
Ұстаз	Ustaz	Teacher
Ұстара	Ustara	Razor
Ұсыну	Usınu	Recomment
Ұшақ	Uşaq	Airplane
Ұшқыш	Uşqış	Plane

113

Kazakh	Transliteration	English
Ұ		
Ұшу	Uşu	Fly
Ұшып кету	Uşıp ketu	Departure
Ұялған	Uyalğan	Embarrassed
Ұялшақ	Uyalşaq	Shy
Ұялы телефон	Uyalı telefon	Mobile phone
Ф		
Ферма	Ferma	Farm
Фото жасау	Foto jasaw	Take photos
Фотограф	Fotograf	Photographer
Фотосурет	Fotosuret	Photo
Фургон	Furgon	Van
Футболка	Futbolka	T-shirt
Х		
Хабар, хат	Xabar, xat	Message
Хайуанаттар бағы	Xaywanattar bağı	Zoo
Ханым	Xanım	Miss (lady)
Ханым	Xanım	Mrs./Ms
Хат	Xat	Letter (envelope)
Хауыз	Xawız	Pool (basin)
Ц		
Цент	Cent	Cent
Цикл	Cïkl	Cycle

Kazakh	Transliteration	English
Ш		
Шабдалы	Şabdalı	Peach
Шайпұл	Şaypul	Tip (tipping)
Шақыру	Şaqıru	Call
Шақыру	Şaqıru	Invite
Шақырым	Şaqırım	Kilometer
Шалбар	Şalbar	Pants (slacks)
Шам	Şam	Bra
Шамдар	Şamdar	Headlights
Шанышқы	Şanışqı	Fork
Шарап	Şarap	Wine
Шаршау	Şarşaw	Tired
Шаш	Şaş	Hair
Шаш алдыру	Şaş aldıru	Haircut
Шәй	Şäy	Tea
Шәй қасық	Şäy qasıq	Teaspoon
Шәйнек	Şäynek	Pot (kettle)
Шелек	Şelek	Bucket
Шетел	Şetel	Overseas
Шешу	Şeşu	Decide
Шие	Şie	Cherry
Шикізат	Şïkizat	Raw
Ширек	Şïrek	Quarter
Шілтер	Şilter	Lace
Шоколад	Şokolad	Chocolate
Шолақ шалбар	Şolaq şalbar	Shorts
Шолу	Şolu	Review

Kazakh	Transliteration	English
Ш		
Шомылатын киім	Şomılatın kïim	Bathing suit
Шомылу киімі	Şomılu kïimi	Swimsuit
Шошқа	Şoşqa	Pig
Шошқа еті	Şoşqa eti	Pork
Шөл	Şöl	Dessert
Шөлдеу	Şöldew	Thirsty (parched)
Шөп	Şöp	Grass
Шөп	Şöp	Herb
Шөпті	Şöpti	Herbal
Штепсель	Ştepsel'	Plug (socket)
Штопор	Ştopor	Bottle opener (corkscrew)
Шуақты	Şuaqtı	Sunny
Шулы	Şulı	Noisy
Шүмек	Şümek	Tap
Шұлықтар	Şulıqtar	Socks
Шығу	Şığu	Exit
Шығу қақпасы	Şığu qaqpası	Departure gate
Шығу, түсу	Şığu, tüsu	Get off (disembark)
Шығыс	Şığıs	East
Шылым	Şılım	Cigarette
Шылым шегуге болмайды	Şılım şeguge bolmaydı	Nonsmoking
Шырын	Şırın	Juice
Щётке	Şçyotke	Brush

Kazakh	Transliteration	English
Ы		
Ыдыс	Idıs	Bowl
Ыдыс	Idıs	Dish
Ыдыс	Idıs	Jar
Ыдыс-аяқ сүрткіш	Idıs-ayaq sürtkiş	Wash cloth
Ызалы	Izalı	Angry
Ылғал	Ilğal	Humid
Ылғал, дымқыл	Ilğal, dımqıl	Wet
Ыңғайлы	Iñğaylı	Comfortable
Ыңғайсыз	Iñğaysız	Uncomfortable
Ырғақ	Irğaq	Rhythm
Ыстық	Istıq	Hot
Ыстық су	Istıq su	Hot water
Э		
Элеватор	Élevator	Elevator
Электр желісі	Élektr jelisi	Electricity
Эскалатор	Éskalator	Escalator

1. Monday
2. Tuesday
3. Wednesday — среда   1pm - 3pm.
4. Thursday
5. Friday
6. Saturday
7. Sunday

Gulnash Askhat

Вашингтон –Алматы
21.05 –03.00.   20 z 55 в пути
27 август   29 август 1 пересдача

9 781522 732433